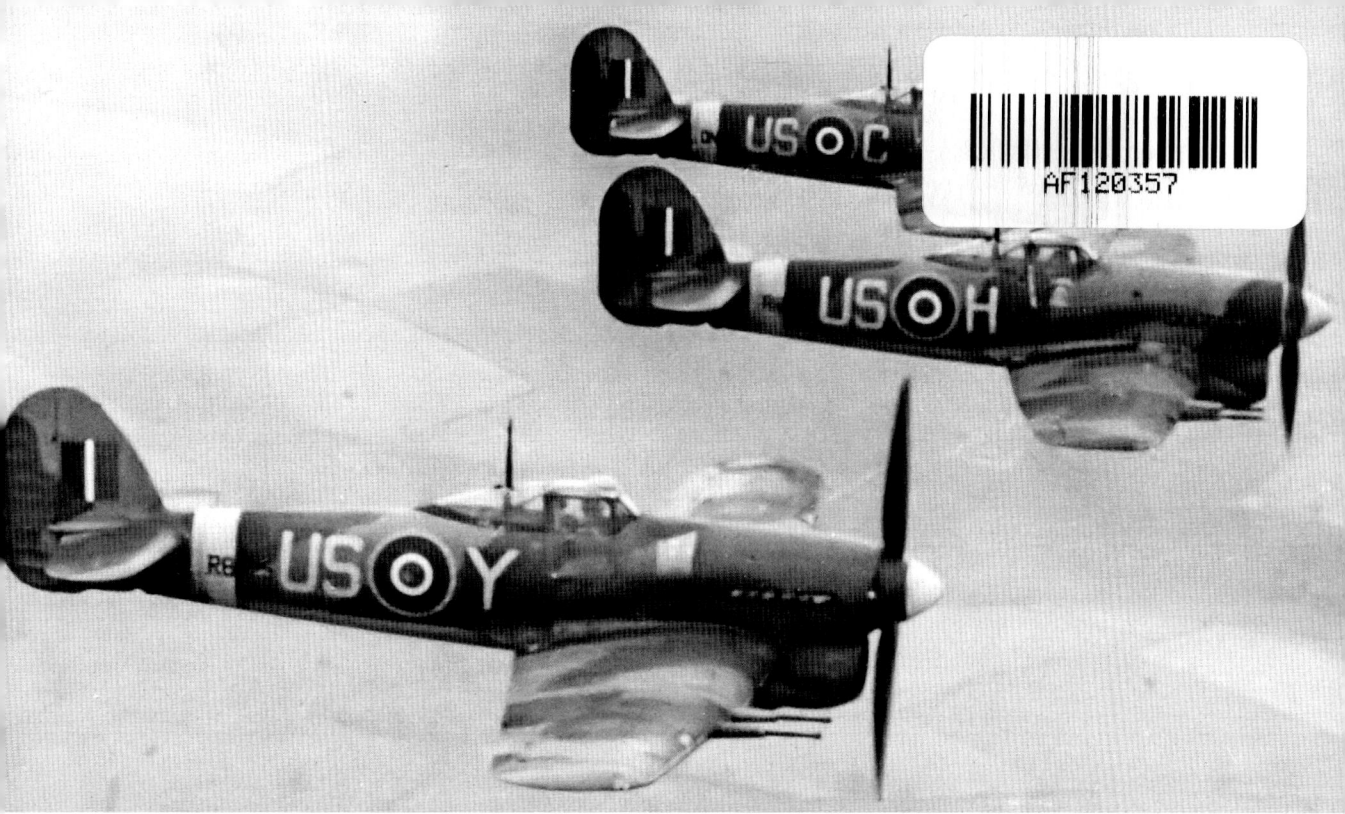

AIR CAMPAIGN

OPERATION CROSSBOW 1943–44

Hunting Hitler's V-weapons

STEVEN J. ZALOGA | ILLUSTRATED BY GRAHAM TURNER

OSPREY PUBLISHING
Bloomsbury Publishing Plc

Kemp House, Chawley Park, Cumnor Hill, Oxford OX2 9PH, UK
29 Earlsfort Terrace, Dublin 2, Ireland
1385 Broadway, 5th Floor, New York, NY 10018, USA
Email: info@ospreypublishing.com
www.ospreypublishing.com

OSPREY is a trademark of Osprey Publishing Ltd

First published in Great Britain in 2018

© Osprey Publishing Ltd, 2018

Transferred to digital print on demand in 2023

All rights reserved. No part of this publication may be reproduced or transmitted in any form or by any means, electronic or mechanical, including photocopying, recording, or any information storage or retrieval system, without prior permission in writing from the publishers.

A catalog record for this book is available from the British Library.

Print ISBN: 978 1 4728 2614 5
eBook: 978 1 4728 2613 8
ePDF: 978 1 4728 2615 2
XML: 978 1 4728 2616 9

Maps by www.bounford.com
3D BEVs by The Black Spot
Index by Rob Munro
Typeset by PDQ Digital Media Solutions, Bungay, UK
Printed and Bound by Intellicor, LLC USA.

The Woodland Trust
Osprey Publishing supports the Woodland Trust, the UK's leading woodland conservation charity.

Artist's note
Readers may care to note that the original paintings from which the color plates in this book were prepared are available for private sale. All reproduction copyright whatsoever is retained by the publishers. All inquiries should be addressed to:

Graham Turner, PO Box 568, Aylesbury, Bucks, HP17 8ZX, UK

Visit the artist's website: www.studio88.co.uk

The publishers regret that they can enter into no correspondence upon this matter.

Image acknowledgments
Front Cover: Art by Graham Turner © Osprey Publishing Ltd
Back Cover: Photo courtesy of author

www.ospreypublishing.com
To find out more about our authors and books visit our website. Here you will find extracts, author interviews, details of forthcoming events and the option to sign-up for our newsletter.

Author's note
The author would like to thank Aldon P. Ferguson of the Burtonwood Association, Dana Bell, and Nick Spark for their help on this project. Unless otherwise noted, the photos in this book are all from the author's collection. With the exception of contemporary photos taken by the author, they are from official US government sources, including the US National Archives and Records Administration, US Army Military History Institute, and the Library of Congress.

Glossary

A-4	Service designation for V-2 ballistic missile
AAF	US Army Air Force
CBO	Combined Bomber Offensive
CIU	Central Interpretation Unit
FR.155W	Flak-Regiment.155W (Werfer)
FZG.76	Flakzielgerät: Antiaircraft target drone, also called V-1
GP	General purpose (bomb)
HDP	Hochdruckpumpe: high-pressure pump, also called V-3
Heavy Crossbow	Fortified missile bunkers
Noball	Allied codename for Crossbow target
OKW	Oberkommando der Wehrmacht: Armed Forces High Command
P20	Peenemünde object with 20-foot wingspan (V-1)
P30, P40	Peenemünde object with 30- or 40-foot length (V-2)
RCAF	Royal Canadian Air Force
Ton	US ton (2,000 pounds)
Tonne	Metric ton (2,204 pounds)
USSTAF	US Strategic Air Forces in Europe
V-1	Vergeltungswaffe-1: Retaliation weapon-1

AIR CAMPAIGN

CONTENTS

INTRODUCTION	4
CHRONOLOGY	6
ATTACKERS' CAPABILITIES	7
DEFENDERS' CAPABILITIES	20
CAMPAIGN OBJECTIVES	29
THE CAMPAIGN	31
ANALYSIS AND CONCLUSION	86
FURTHER READING	93
INDEX	95

INTRODUCTION

An FZG.76 cruise missile on its Walter 2.3 catapult ramp, currently preserved at the Watten museum on the Pas-de-Calais.

The Luftwaffe had failed in its plans to subdue Britain by air attack in 1940. Infuriated by the rising crescendo of RAF bomber attacks on German cities in 1943, Hitler turned to exotic new "Vengeance" weapons to turn the tide of war. Operation *Eisbär* (Polar Bear) was scheduled to start on December 1, 1943 with the aim of devastating London with a combined attack of FZG.76 cruise missiles, A-4 ballistic missiles, and the HDP (Hochdruckpumpe: high-pressure pump) long-range gun.

Operation *Eisbär* was primarily intended by Hitler as a retaliatory campaign against Britain in response to RAF Bomber Command's escalating attacks against German cities. The RAF was conducting heavy bomber missions on a scale impossible for the Luftwaffe to counter. A few statistics help elucidate this point. The British air campaign against the Ruhr industrial region from March 1 to July 31, 1943 included about 19,600 sorties dropping 43,990 tons of bombs, killing 21,880 people and destroying 57,235 buildings. The subsequent campaign against Berlin from November 18, 1943 to March 24, 1944 involved 8,495 sorties dropping 29,785 tons of bombs, killing about 6,000 people and destroying 26,700 buildings. By way of comparison, the Luftwaffe bombing attacks on Britain in 1943 consisted of only 33 raids involving about 1,945 sorties dropping 1,975 tonnes of bombs.

Hitler vaguely hoped that the scale of destruction wreaked by the missile campaign would be sufficient to turn the tide of war. How he expected to accomplish this is unrecorded since the scale of the missile attacks, even in the most optimistic plans, was far short of the tonnage dropped on Germany by RAF Bomber Command and the US Strategic Air Forces. Regardless of whether Hitler genuinely believed that the V-weapon offensive could change the course of the war, it became a central feature of German propaganda in 1944.

The relative importance of Operation *Eisbär* increased through early 1944 owing to the failure of the Luftwaffe's parallel bombing campaign, Operation *Steinbock*. This bomber offensive, sometimes dubbed the "Baby Blitz," was launched in January 1944 as another dimension in Germany's retaliatory campaign against Britain. Luftflotte 3 started the campaign with about 475 bombers. The campaign eventually totaled 31 raids and 4,218 sorties with 329 aircraft losses by the time it ended in May 1944. The raids delivered 2,795 tons of bombs, but only about 930 tons were dropped against their intended targets due to the effectiveness of British air defenses. In view of the Luftwaffe's failure to conduct a retaliatory campaign using traditional means, Hitler hoped that Operation *Eisbär* would succeed using the revolutionary new technology.

The plans for Operation *Eisbär* anticipated a monthly production rate by the summer of 1944 of 6,000 FZG.76 cruise missiles and about 1,000 A-4 ballistic missiles. This implies a maximum potential delivery of about 10,000 tonnes against London monthly, about five times the scale of the entire Operation *Steinbock* campaign in 1944. In September 1944, Hitler increased the monthly production goals to 9,000 FZG.76 and 2,000 A-4 missiles, though in reality they never exceeded 3,420 FZG.76 and 360 A-4 missiles.

The range of these weapons inevitably meant that they would be launched from near the British coast and so within the striking range of Allied bombers. British intelligence successes led to the discovery of the missile program months before they were ready for combat. Operation *Crossbow*, a preemptive bomber campaign, was launched against the missile sites in France in the fall and winter of 1943. This derailed the original German scheme to start the attacks in December 1943 and forced the adoption of new basing modes for the V-weapons.

Although the new sites proved to be less vulnerable to air attack than the initial launch sites, they were also considerably less efficient. Operation *Eisbär* was finally launched on the night of June 12/13, 1944, more than six months behind schedule. This was the first major missile campaign in history. The attacks led to a political crisis in London due to the escalating civilian casualties, with demands that the Allied air forces stop the attacks. Phase II of Operation *Crossbow* was driven by political considerations and caused a sizable diversion of RAF Bomber Command during the critical summer months of 1944. There was intense and bitter debate among the British and American "bomber barons" over the proper tactics to deal with the missile threat. Later assessments criticized the summer campaign for its extravagant use of heavy bombing without commensurate results in dampening the missile attacks. Other defensive efforts such as an antiaircraft gun belt and expanded fighter defense of London had a more significant effect on lessening the attack of the "Doodlebugs." This book focuses on the *Crossbow* bomber campaign against the German missile threat. The story of the RAF fighter defense of London against the Doodlebugs has been detailed in other Osprey books.[1] The V-1 launch sites in France and Belgium were overrun by Canadian and British forces in the late summer of 1944, ending Operation *Crossbow*. The V-2 ballistic missile belatedly emerged in the fall of 1944, fired from mobile launchers in the Netherlands. Countermeasures against these later attacks fall outside the scope of Operation *Crossbow*.

In spite of their feeble results, the V-weapons were the ancestors of the Cold War's awesome nuclear missiles. Their launch sites served as a guide for later missile launch complexes. The lessons of the first missile campaign were not forgotten, and the V-2 served as inspiration to the infamous Scud missile so prominent in Mid-East wars in the last two decades of the 20th century.

---

1   Andrew Thomas, *V1 Flying Bomb Aces (Osprey Aircraft of the Aces 113: 2013); Meteor I vs V1 Flying Bomb (Osprey Duel 45: 2012).*

CHRONOLOGY

1943

July 12 First RAF photo mission over Peenemünde to discover a missile

August 1 Flak-Regiment.155W established at Zempin

August 17/18 RAF stages Operation *Hydra* raid on Peenemünde

August 27 Eighth Air Force raid on Watten Heavy Crossbow site

September 26 First 51 pre-series FZG.76 delivered to Peenemünde

October 16 First launch of FZG.76 missile from Zempin by FR.155W

October 21 I./FR.155W dispatched to France

October 22 RAF raid shuts down first FZG.76 assembly line in Kassel

November 18 Last of FW.155W launch batteries departs Zempin for France

November 28 RAF photo mission over Peenemünde discovers FZG.76

December 1 Planned start of Operation *Eisbär*

December 5 First wave of *Crossbow* attacks

December 15 FR.155W headquarters arrives in France

December 24 First large *Crossbow* Phase I raid, aka Plan Eye-Que

1944

February 10–24 *Crossbow* tests at Eglin Proving Ground

June 6 Rumpelkammer preparation phase initiated in response to D-Day landings

June 12/13 Operation *Eisbär* begins prematurely

June 15/16 First successful mass FZG.76 launch

June 19 First Tallboy attack on Heavy Crossbow site

June 20 Eighth Air Force raid on FZG.76 plant in Fallersleben

July 9 First air launch of FZG.76 against London

August 4 First Aphrodite attack on Heavy Crossbow site

August 8 IV./FR.155W withdrawn from service

September 1 Last FZG.76 launch by FR.155W from France

September 3 First A-4/V-2 launch against London

ATTACKERS' CAPABILITIES
Allied air forces' power in England, 1943–44

Intelligence

Britain's first line of defense against the German missile threat was its vigorous intelligence effort. Since 1940, British intelligence agencies had collected a variety of reports, some of them fanciful, about German secret weapons campaigns. The most important, dubbed the "Oslo report" came from disgruntled German physicist Hans Ferdinand Mayer in November 1939 who provided the British embassy with an overview of early German missile development. Traditional espionage was supplemented by newer intelligence methods, including photographic reconnaissance and signals intelligence.

Due to extensive new construction work, the Peenemünde development center became the target of RAF photo reconnaissance flights in January 1943. The Central Interpretation Unit (CIU), based at RAF Medmenham, was Britain's center for photographic intelligence. On April 20, 1943, the Minister of Supply and Churchill's son-in-law, Duncan Sandys, was appointed to lead the Bodyline Committee, tasked with keeping track of the growing number of reports about missile weapons. The first critical breakthrough in the missile campaign was the July 12, 1943 mission over Peenemünde that revealed an A-4 missile on its transport trailer near its test stand. A follow-on mission by a Mosquito with better cameras on July 23, 1943 exposed the FZG.76 for the first time, but it was not immediately recognized. Besides the growing photographic evidence, other sources about Peenemünde began to emerge. Foreign workers who had been involved in construction began to report to local resistance groups about the rocket work. There were still skeptics among Churchill's advisers, notably Lord Cherwell (F.A. Lindemann) who famously observed that once the war had ended, the reports of large missiles would prove to be nothing more than "a mare's nest." By the end of July 1943, a consensus had emerged among British intelligence analysts that the German ballistic missile, dubbed P30, did in fact exist. Indeed, the conviction was strong enough that RAF Bomber Command staged Operation *Hydra*,

The backbone of the Ninth Air Force's effort during Operation *Crossbow* was its B-26 squadrons. This is a pair of B-26B Marauders of the 449th BS, 322nd Bomb Group during a mission to Saint Omer and Fort Rouge in 1943.

its first raid on Peenemünde, on the night of August 17/18, 1943. The raid was not as destructive as Churchill might have hoped, but it did impose delays on the A-4 ballistic missile program.

Further evidence of the German missile program continued to accumulate in the fall of 1943. The plausibility of a winged missile was confirmed in late August 1943 when the Luftwaffe began employing its Henschel Hs.293 antiship missile in the Mediterranean theater. It was significantly smaller than the FZG.76, but made it abundantly clear that the Luftwaffe was developing winged cruise missiles. An FZG.76 fired by FR.155W from the training site at Zempin landed on Bornholm Island in Denmark, and a sketch of the missile arrived in Britain. The first reports began to emerge from France about the construction of large concrete structures on the Pas-de-Calais that seemed to have no apparent connection to the Atlantic Wall fortification program. There was growing reason to believe that these were the first signs of German missile bases. Photographic reconnaissance missions, dubbed Rhubarb, were conducted over areas in France and Germany associated with the missile mystery. Imagery from a November 28, 1943 flight over Zempin finally disclosed the enigmatic "P20" cruise missile on its launch ramp.

The growing volume of evidence led to reconfiguration of Sandys' Bodyline committee as a new subcommittee to the Joint Intelligence Committee, codenamed *Crossbow* at Churchill's suggestion. Still led by Sandys, the *Crossbow* committee included other key players in the unfolding drama, including the perceptive scientist R.V. Jones, head of the Scientific Section of MI6. Jones had a far clearer appreciation of the means of technical intelligence and had requested that British signals intelligence pay special attention to a Luftwaffe signals regiment operating in the Peenemünde area. He presumed that these teams would use radar to track the test missiles, and there might be the added bonus of telemetry signals or radio guidance signals. Indeed, by December, extensive data had been obtained which provided specific evidence of the range of the "P20," by now known to be called FZG.76 from other signals intelligence collection.

The success of British intelligence in uncovering the German secret missile program was instrumental in derailing the early deployment of the A-4 ballistic missile. This is a photo of the P-7 test site at Peenemünde taken on June 23, 1943 from the Mosquito piloted by Flight Sergeant E.P.H. Peak. An A-4 missile on its transporter is labeled (A), the gantry towers (B), and the assembly hall (C). Two more A-4 missiles can be seen on their trailers at the entrance to the protective berm around the launch site.

This is an aerial reconnaissance photo taken on November 9, 1943 showing the "ski site" at Yvrench, northeast of Abbeville, later given the intelligence designation Noball XI/A/25. The building in the foreground is a ski-shaped Vorratslager, after which these sites were named. The Luftwaffe decision to use a stereotyped launch site configuration made it easier for British intelligence to identify the ski sites.

Aside from more detailed information on the performance of the P20 and P30, British intelligence had little or no information on their basing mode. There were some suggestions that the ballistic missile might need a huge mortar tube or some form of inclined ramp. The first hints of the missile bases on the Pas-de-Calais began to emerge in April 1943 when reconnaissance aircraft were conducting periodic photo missions. The site at Watten naturally attracted attention owing to its sheer size. Lt. Gen. Lewis Brereton, US Ninth Air Force commander, described it as "more extensive than any concrete constructions we have in the United States with the possible exception of the Boulder Dam." By mid-July 1944, the layout had grown to 330x460 feet and there were about 6,000 workers on site. The structure did not seem to have any normal military function, so it was quickly presumed that it had something to do with the "rocket gun" threat. Work also escalated at the nearby Wizernes limestone quarry, with some 35,000 workers eventually involved in carving out its numerous storage tunnels.

The first Allied mission of what eventually became labeled Operation *Crossbow* was conducted on August 27, 1943 against Watten's "concrete monster." There was some recognition that ordinary high explosive bombs were not effective in penetrating thick steel-reinforced concrete. As a result, the US Eighth Air Force consulted British civil engineers who suggested that the ideal time to bomb the site would be after extensive concrete pours but before the concrete had time to harden. This determined the time frame of the mission. The attack on August 27, 1943 was conducted in the early evening by 224 B-17 bombers of the 1st and 4th Bomb Wings totaling 368 2,000lb general purpose bombs. Local Luftwaffe air units intercepted the mission and a total of four B-17 bombers were lost with claims of seven German fighters destroyed. The attack was entirely successful, though this was not fully appreciated at the time. As expected, the damage caused by heavy bombs against uncured concrete created extensive damage to the structure. At first, the German engineers felt that the damage could be repaired in three or four months. In the event, the damage was so severe that the bunker was never constructed as intended. The final construction was limited to a liquid oxygen generation station with no missile launch facility. Instead, the Wizernes quarry site was reconfigured for missile launch under a massive concrete dome. The heavy bombers of the US Eighth Air Force returned to Watten several times that fall, eventually halting any significant construction work. Berlin decided to continue modest work at the site to divert Allied bombers from more worthwhile targets.

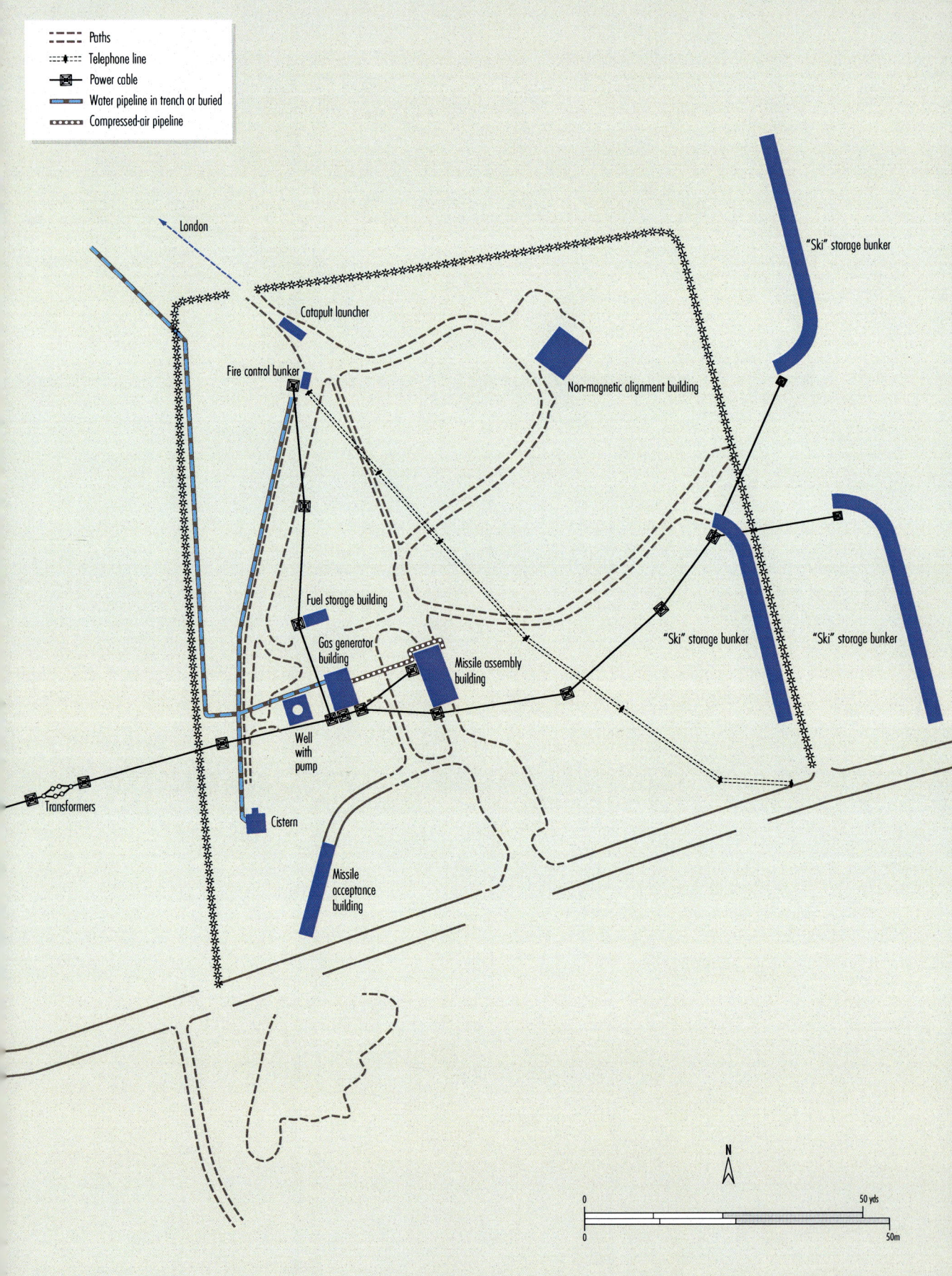

OPPOSITE V-1 SKI SITE LAYOUT (YVRENCH/BOIS CARRÉ)

In October 1943, French resistance networks reported that construction was under way at six or more sites consisting of a concrete runway apparently aimed at London along with several buildings. This prompted Sandys to request a thorough photo reconnaissance survey of the Pas-de-Calais that started on October 28 and eventually totaled over a hundred sorties. By November, French sources had identified more than 70 sites. Photo interpreters had a hard time categorizing the sites, because it had been presumed that they would be near a major railway in order to handle the delivery of a multi-ton ballistic missile. Instead, the sites were located in rural farmland with modest road networks. By early November 1943, it was obvious that these sites were of a stereotyped layout and that they were readily identifiable by the presence of three "J"-shaped buildings, which one analyst described as shaped like skis. Since the first site was located near Bois Carré, they were initially called Bois Carré or ski sites. By November 7, 1943, some 19 ski sites had been identified and additional sites seemed to accumulate with every photo reconnaissance mission. By the end of the year, 96 had been identified, primarily in the Pas-de-Calais area aimed at London, but with a smaller number on the Cotentin Peninsula near Cherbourg facing Portsmouth. Eventually, it was realized that the layout of the Bois Carré sites mirrored the Zempin training site near Peenemünde. This provided conclusive evidence that the ski sites were intended for use with the P20 flying bomb.

The crew of a B-17F (42-31135) of the 562nd BS, 388th Bombardment Group are briefed for Noball Mission 221 over France on February 13, 1944. The officers in the center looking at the map (left to right) are bombardier 1Lt. Richard Donner, pilot 1Lt Dan Sullivan, and co-pilot 2Lt Robert Zapp.

ATTACKERS' CAPABILITIES

The senior Allied bomber commanders in 1943 were Air Chief Marshal Sir Arthur Harris (left) leading RAF Bomber Command, and Maj. Gen. Ira Eaker (right) leading the Eighth Air Force. Eaker was forced out with the arrival of Gen. Dwight D. Eisenhower's Mediterranean veterans, with Carl Spaatz appointed to the new USSTAF command, and James Doolittle taking over the Eighth Air Force.

Leader of the Eighth Air Force starting in January 1944 was Lt. Gen. James "Jimmy" Doolittle, previously the commander of the Fifteenth Air Force in the Mediterranean Theater, and leader of the legendary raid on Tokyo in 1942.

Aircraft

By this stage of the war, the Allies had a very substantial strike force capable of attacking the "Rocket Gun Coast." This consisted primarily of two heavy bomber forces and two tactical air forces equipped with medium bombers and fighter bombers. RAF Bomber Command, commanded by Air Chief Marshal Sir Arthur Harris, was Britain's strategic bomber arm. Over the course of the war, it had evolved into a force primarily aimed at conducting night bombing missions. Its American counterpart was the US Strategic Air Forces in Europe (USSTAF), commanded by Gen. Carl Spaatz. This consisted of the Eighth Air Force based in Britain under the command of Lt. Gen. James H. Doolittle and the Fifteenth Air Force based in Italy under the command of Maj. Gen. Nathan F. Twining. The USSTAF included heavy bombers as well as escorting day fighters.

At the end of 1943, both RAF Bomber Command and USSTAF were heavily committed to the Combined Bomber Offensive (CBO). The CBO name papered over the fundamental disagreement between the RAF and AAF (US Army Air Force) over the conduct of the strategic bombing campaign. Harris insisted that night area attacks on German cities would lead to a collapse of German civilian morale and destroy enough housing to seriously impact German industry.

Air Chief Marshal Sir Trafford Leigh-Mallory led the Allied Expeditionary Air Force that was nominally in control of Operation *Crossbow*. He ran into resistance from the "bomber barons" including Harris and Spaatz and was eventually forced out of the *Crossbow* mission.

The AAF was convinced that daylight precision bombing of German industry was a more effective approach. Operation *Pointblank*, initiated by the USSTAF in the fall of 1943, tried to narrow the focus of the strategic bombing campaign towards the goal of defeating the Luftwaffe fighter force. The AAF took up the *Pointblank* mission with enthusiasm, since US doctrine considered the defeat of the Luftwaffe an essential prelude to a broader campaign against German war industries. The senior Allied army commanders wanted the Luftwaffe suppressed prior to the start of Operation *Overlord*, the Normandy amphibious landings, scheduled for the late spring of 1944, and so supported the *Pointblank* plan.

The RAF's 2nd Tactical Air Force, commanded by Air Marshal Sir Arthur Coningham, contained the medium bombers, fighter bombers, and fighters that would provide air support to the Allied armies in the field. As of November 1943, it included three groups: 2 Group based in Norfolk with 12 medium and light bomber squadrons, 83 Group in Surrey with 21 fighter squadrons, and 84 Group in Oxford with 20 fighter and fighter-bomber squadrons.

Its American counterpart was the Ninth Air Force, commanded by Lt. Gen. Lewis Brereton. In early 1944, this consisted of three principal elements. IX Bomber Command with seven medium bomber squadrons, IX Fighter Command with eight fighter squadrons, and IX Troop Carrier Command with five transport squadrons. This order of battle increased dramatically by the time of D-Day to 11 medium bomber squadrons, 18 fighter squadrons, and 14 transport squadrons.

These tactical air forces were engaged in a variety of missions over France prior to the Operation *Overlord* landings in Normandy on June 6, 1944. These included fighter sweeps directed against Luftwaffe fighter squadrons in France and Belgium, as well as bombing missions against a wide variety of targets such as railways, German depots, maritime traffic, and targets outlined in the *Overlord* plans. The two tactical air forces began to be committed to Operation *Crossbow* on November 5, 1943, and this mission eventually came to absorb a substantial fraction of overall sorties through the start of the Normandy campaign in June 1944.

ATTACKERS' CAPABILITIES

RAF BOMBER COMMAND BOMBER UNITS, JUNE 1944*		
1 Group		
12 Squadron	Lancaster	Wickenby
100 Squadron	Lancaster	Waltham
101 Squadron	Lancaster	Ludford Magna
103 Squadron	Lancaster	Elsham Wolds
166 Squadron	Lancaster	Kirmington
300 Squadron	Lancaster	Faldingworth
460 Squadron	Lancaster	Binbrook
550 Squadron	Lancaster	North Killingholme
576 Squadron	Lancaster	Elsham Wolds
625 Squadron	Lancaster	Kelstern
626 Squadron	Lancaster	Wickenby
3 Group		
15 Squadron	Lancaster	Mildenhall
75 Squadron	Lancaster	Mepal
90 Squadron	Lancaster	Tuddenham
115 Squadron	Lancaster	Witchford
138 (Special Duty) Squadron	Halifax, Stirling	Tempsford
149 Squadron	Lancaster	Methwold
161 (Special Duty) Squadron	Halifax	Tempsford
218 Squadron	Lancaster	Woolfox Lodge
514 Squadron	Lancaster	Witchford
622 Squadron	Lancaster	Mildenhall
4 Group		
10 Squadron	Halifax	Melbourne
51 Squadron	Halifax	Snaith
76 Squadron	Halifax	Holme-on-Spalding Moor
78 Squadron	Halifax	Breighton
102 Squadron	Halifax	Pocklington
158 Squadron	Halifax	Lisset
346 Squadron	Halifax	Elvington
466 Squadron	Halifax	Driffield
578 Squadron	Halifax	Burn
640 Squadron	Halifax	Leconfield
5 Group		
9 Squadron	Lancaster	Bardney
44 Squadron	Lancaster	Dunholme Lodge
49 Squadron	Lancaster	Fiskerton
50 Squadron	Lancaster	Skellingthorpe
57 Squadron	Lancaster	East Kirkby
61 Squadron	Lancaster	Skellingthorpe
83 Squadron	Lancaster	Coningsby
97 Squadron	Lancaster	Coningsby
106 Squadron	Lancaster	Metheringham
207 Squadron	Lancaster	Spilsby
463 Squadron	Lancaster	Waddington
467 Squadron	Lancaster	Waddington
617 Squadron	Lancaster	Woodhall Spa
627 Squadron	Lancaster	Woodhall Spa

630 Squadron	Lancaster	East Kirkby
691 Squadron	Lancaster	Dunholme Lodge
6 Group (RCAF)		
408 Squadron	Lancaster	Linton-on-Ouse
419 Squadron	Lancaster	Middleton St. George
420 Squadron	Halifax	Tholthorpe
424 Squadron	Lancaster	Skipton-on-Swale
425 Squadron	Halifax	Tholthorpe
426 Squadron	Halifax	Linton-on-Ouse
427 Squadron	Halifax	Leeming
428 Squadron	Lancaster	Middleton St. George
429 Squadron	Halifax	Leemings
431 Squadron	Halifax	East Moor
433 Squadron	Halifax	Skipton on Swale
434 Squadron	Halifax	East Moor
*Does not include Pathfinder Group or 100 (BS) Group		

EIGHTH AIR FORCE HEAVY BOMBER STRENGTH, JANUARY–MAY 1944						
Month	B-17 Available	B-24 Available	Available Subtotal	B-17 Operational	B-24 Operational	Operational Subtotal
January	938	244	1,182	657	186	843
February	1,129	352	1,481	786	260	1,046
March	1,100	399	1,499	792	302	1,094
April	1,129	485	1,614	908	379	1,287
May	1,190	836	2,026	949	675	1,624

The main contributors to the Ninth Air Force's role in Operation *Crossbow* were the A-20 and B-26 medium bombers. This is a trio of A-20 of the 668th BS, 416th Bomb Group on a Noball mission over the Pas-de-Calais.

ATTACKERS' CAPABILITIES

USAAF EIGHTH AIR FORCE BOMBER UNITS, JUNE 1944		
1st Bombardment Division		
1st Bombardment Wing		
91st Bombardment Group	B-17	Bassingbourn
381st Bombardment Group	B-17	Ridgewell
398th Bombardment Group	B-17	Nuthampstead
40th Bombardment Wing		
92nd Bombardment Group	B-17	Podington
305th Bombardment Group	B-17	Chelveston
306th Bombardment Group	B-17	Thurleigh
41st Bombardment Wing		
303rd Bombardment Group	B-17	Molesworth
379th Bombardment Group	B-17	Kimbolton
384th Bombardment Group	B-17	Grafton Underwood
94th Bombardment Wing		
351st Bombardment Group	B-17	Polebrook
401st Bombardment Group	B-17	Deenethorpe
457th Bombardment Group	B-17	Glatton
2nd Bombardment Division		
2nd Bombardment Wing		
389th Bombardment Group	B-24	Hethel
445th Bombardment Group	B-24	Tibenham
453rd Bombardment Group	B-24	Old Buckenham
14th Bombardment Wing		
44th Bombardment Group	B-24	Shipdham
392nd Bombardment Group	B-24	Wendling
492nd Bombardment Group	B-24	North Pickenham
20th Bombardment Wing		
93rd Bombardment Group	B-24	Hardwick
446th Bombardment Group	B-24	Bungay
448th Bombardment Group	B-24	Seething
95th Bombardment Wing		
489th Bombardment Group	B-24	Halesworth
491st Bombardment Group	B-24	Metfield
96th Bombardment Wing		
458th Bombardment Group	B-24	Horsham St. Faith
466th Bombardment Group	B-24	Attlebridge
467th Bombardment Group	B-24	Rackheath
3rd Bombardment Division		
4th Bombardment Wing		
94th Bombardment Group	B-17	Bury St. Edmunds
385th Bombardment Group	B-17	Great Ashfield
447th Bombardment Group	B-17	Rattlesden
13th Bombardment Wing		
95th Bombardment Group	B-17	Horham
100th Bombardment Group	B-17	Thorpe Abbotts
390th Bombardment Group	B-17	Framlingham
45th Bombardment Wing		
96th Bombardment Group	B-17	Snetterton Heath
388th Bombardment Group	B-17	Knettishall

452nd Bombardment Group	B-17	Deopham Green
92nd Bombardment Wing		
486th Bombardment Group	B-17	Sudbury
487th Bombardment Group	B-17	Lavenham
93rd Bombardment Wing		
34th Bombardment Group	B-17	Mendlesham
490th Bombardment Group	B-17	Eye
493rd Bombardment Group	B-17	Debach

RAF 2ND TACTICAL AIR FORCE, JUNE 1944		
34(PR) Wing		
16, 69, 140 Squadrons	Spitfire, Wellington, Mosquito	Northolt
2 Group		
137 Wing		
88, 226, 342 Squadrons	Boston, Mitchell	Hartford Bridge
138 Wing		
107, 305(Polish), 613 Squadrons	Mosquito	Lasham
139 Wing		
98, 180, 320(Dutch) Squadrons	Mitchell	Dunsfold
140 Wing		
21, 464(RAAF), 487(RNZAF) Squadrons	Mosquito	Hunsdon
83 Group		
39(Recce) Wing		
168, 400(RCAF), 414(RCAF), 430(RCAF) Squadrons	Mustang, Spitfire	Odiham
121 Wing		
174, 175, 245 Squadrons	Typhoon	Holmsley South
122 Wing		
19, 65, 122 Squadrons	Mustang	Funtington
124 Wing		
181, 182, 247 Squadrons	Typhoon	Hurn
125 Wing		
132, 453(RAAF), 602 Squadrons	Spitfire	Ford
126 Wing		
401(RCAF), 411(RCAF), 412(RCAF) Squadrons	Spitfire	Tangmere
127 Wing		
403(RCAF), 416(RCAF), 421(RCAF) Squadrons	Spitfire	Tangmere
129 Wing		
184 Squadron	Typhoon	Westhampnett
143 Wing		
438(RCAF), 439(RCAF), 440(RCAF) Squadrons	Typhoon	Hurn
144 Wing		
441(RCAF), 442(RCAF), 443(RCAF) Squadrons	Spitfire	Ford
84 Group		
35(Recce) Wing		
2, 4, 268 Squadrons	Mustang, Spitfire	Gatwick
123 Wing		
198, 609 Squadrons	Typhoon	Thorney Island
131 Wing		

ATTACKERS' CAPABILITIES

302(Polish), 308(Polish), 317(Polish) Squadrons	Spitfire	Chailey
132 Wing		
66, 331(Norwegian), 332(Norwegian) Squadrons	Spitfire	Bognor
133 Wing		
129, 306(Polish), 315(Polish) Squadrons	Mustang	Coolham
134 Wing		
310(Czech), 312(Czech), 313(Czech) Squadrons	Spitfire	Appledram
135 Wing		
222, 349(Belgian), 485(RNZAF) Squadrons	Spitfire	Selsey
136 Wing		
164, 184 Squadrons	Typhoon	Thorney Island
145 Wing		
329(French), 340(French), 341(French) Squadrons	Spitfire	Merston
146 Wing		
193, 197, 257, 266 Squadrons	Typhoon	Needs Oar Point
85 Group		
141 Wing		
264, 322(Dutch), 410(RCAF) Squadrons	Mosquito, Spitfire	Hartford Bridge
142 Wing		
124 Squadron	Spitfire	Horne
147 Wing		
488(RNZAF), 604 Squadrons	Mosquito	Zeals
148 Wing		
29, 91, 409(RCAF) Squadrons	Mosquito, Spitfire	West Malling
150 Wing		
3, 56, 486(RNZAF) Squadrons	Tempest, Spitfire	Newchurch
USAAF NINTH AIR FORCE, JUNE 1944*		
IX Fighter Command		
422nd, 423rd, 425th Night Fighter Squadrons	P-61	Middle Wallop
IX Tactical Air Command		
67th Tac Recon Group	F-6	Middle Wallop
70th Fighter Wing		
48th Fighter Group	P-47	Ibsley
367th Fighter Group	P-38	Stoney Cross
371st Fighter Group	P-47	Bisterne
474th Fighter Group	P-38	Warmwell
71st Fighter Wing		
366th Fighter Group	P-47	Thruxton
368th Fighter Group	P-47	Chilbolton
370th Fighter Group	P-38	Andover
84th Fighter Wing		
50th Fighter Group	P-47	Lymington
365th Fighter Group	P-47	Beaulieu
404th Fighter Group	P-47	Winkton
405th Fighter Group	P-47	Christchurch
XIX Tactical Air Command		

10th PR Group	F-5	Chalgrove
100th Fighter Wing		
354th Fighter Group	P-51	Lashenden
358th Fighter Group	P-47	High Halden
362nd Fighter Group	P-47	Wormingford
363rd Fighter Group	P-51	Staplehurst
303rd Fighter Wing		
36th Fighter Group	P-47	Kingsnorth
373rd Fighter Group	P-47	Woodchurch
406th Fighter Group	P-47	Ashford
IX Bomber Command		
1st Pathfinder Squadron	B-26	Great Saling
97th Bomb Wing		
409th Bomb Group	A-20	Little Walden
410th Bomb Group	A-20	Gosfield
416th Bomb Group	A-20	Wethersfield
98th Bomb Wing		
323rd Bomb Group	B-26	Earls Colne
387th Bomb Group	B-26	Chipping Ongar
394th Bomb Group	B-26	Boreham
397th Bomb Group	B-26	Rivenhall
99th Bomb Wing		
322nd Bomb Group	B-26	Andrews Field
344th Bomb Group	B-26	Stansted
386th Bomb Group	B-26	Great Dunmow
391st Bomb Group	B-26	Matching

*IX Troop Carrier Command not listed.

The Air Ministry did not favor the use of fighter bombers to eliminate ski sites due to fear of a high attrition rate to German flak. Instead, the 2nd Tactical Air Force used its fighter bombers to conduct harassment attacks on Crossbow sites after bomber attacks to discourage any further construction or repair. These are a trio of Hawker Typhoon IB of 56 Squadron which served with 2nd Tactical Air Force in Phase I of the *Crossbow* campaign. This squadron converted to Tempest V in June 1944, and subsequently took part in the defense of London against V-1 buzz bombs.

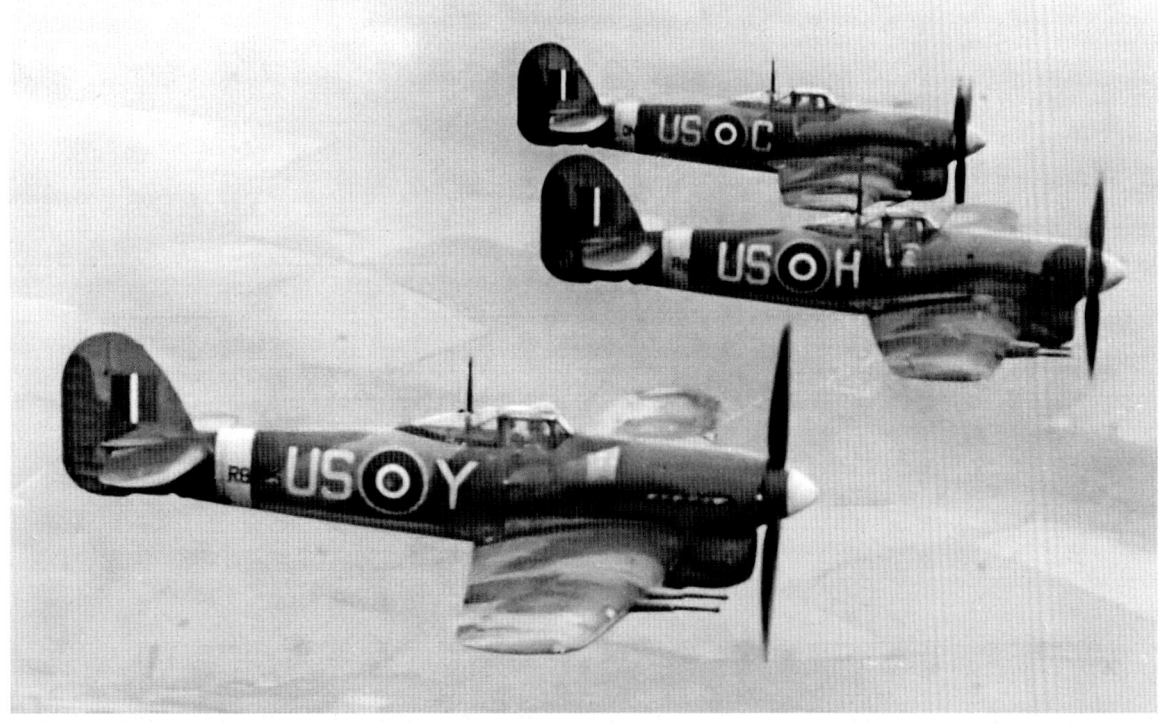

DEFENDERS' CAPABILITIES
The targets and their defenses

The Fieseler Fi-103 cruise missile had a variety of Luftwaffe codenames, starting with FZG.76 and Kirschkern (Cherry pit). On April 30, 1944, Hitler ordered that FZG.76 be dropped in favor of Maikäfer (June Bug). This was a short-lived name once the German propaganda ministry started using the term V-1 (Vergeltungswaffe-1: Retaliation weapon-1) during radio broadcasts on June 23, 1944. V-1 lasted until November 2, 1944 when Hitler renamed it Krähe (Crow).

Commander of Flak-Regiment.155W, Oberst Max Wachtel.

By the summer of 1943, the Wehrmacht was developing a trio of revolutionary new weapons intended to strike at London. The German Army (Heer) had been pursuing two separate programs that were intended to surpass the Paris Gun of the Great War tenfold in range and power. The A-4 Feuerteufel (Fire-devil), better known by its later propaganda designation as the V-2, was the world's first successful ballistic missile. Its first successful test flight was conducted on October 3, 1942, but its technology was immature and took more than a year to reach serial production. The army's other program was more obscure. The HDP (Hochdruckpumpe: high-pressure pump), later called Tausendfüßler (millipede) and V-3, was a multi-barrel gun complex intended to fire about 600 rounds per hour or 20,000 projectiles per month. The German generals promised that the new weapons would succeed where the Luftwaffe had failed in the 1940 Battle of Britain.

The Luftwaffe, unwilling to have its strategic bombardment mission usurped by the army, was developing a less sophisticated and less costly alternative to the A-4, the Fiesler FZG.76 cruise missile, better known as the V-1 buzz bomb. In Luftwaffe service, it was known by various codenames including FZG.76, (Flakzielgerät: antiaircraft target drone) and Kirschkern (cherry pit). The first powered air-launch test was conducted on December 10, 1942 and the first test using a ground catapult took place on December 24, 1942.

On Hitler's orders, a special commission was created on May 26, 1943 to determine whether the Luftwaffe's FZG.76 cruise missile or the army's A-4 ballistic missile was the preferable bombardment weapon. They concluded that both the FZG.76 and

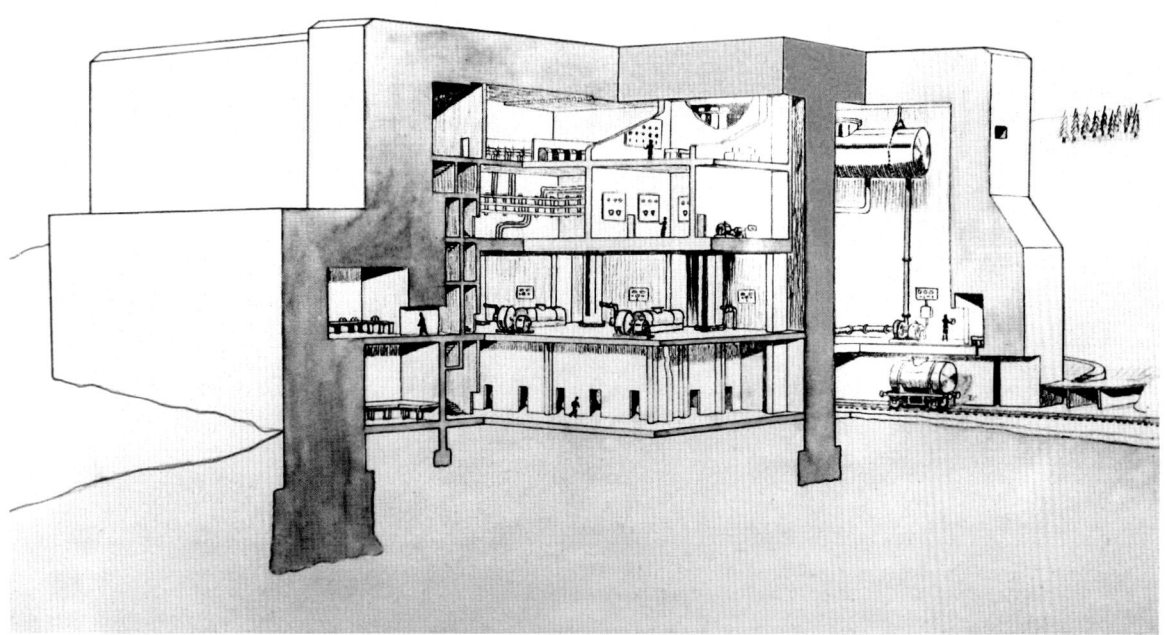

The Kraftwerk Nordwest bunker near Watten was intended to serve as an A-4 missile base complete with its own liquid oxygen plant and missile assembly halls. In the event, Allied bombing attacks destroyed the missile hall and Organization Todt attempted to complete the bunker as a liquid oxygen production factory as seen in this wartime intelligence sketch.

A-4 should be manufactured since they were complementary to one another. The FZG.76 was judged to be more vulnerable to interception but was far less expensive to manufacture and much simpler to operate. The A-4 ballistic missile was invulnerable to interception but was very expensive to manufacture and complicated to operate. The plan was to start the missile offensive, codenamed *Eisbär* (Polar Bear), in December 1943.

Development of the A-4 and FZG.76 missiles was undertaken at a secret facility at Peenemünde on Germany's Baltic coast. British intelligence had picked up faint traces of the program over the years, and photo reconnaissance in 1943 uncovered photos of possible missile test sites at Peenemünde. Although there was no clear appreciation of the exact capabilities of these mystery weapons, RAF Bomber Command staged Operation *Hydra* on the night of August 17/18, 1943 which damaged but did not destroy the test center.

As the new weapons approached serial production, decisions had to be made regarding their deployment. The initial scheme for the A-4 ballistic missile was to create a large bunker in the Pas-de-Calais area on the Channel coast in France where the missiles could be assembled and prepared for launch. The A-4 used liquid oxygen as one of its propellants, and the most efficient method for large-scale launches was to produce liquid oxygen on site using industrial compressors. The compressors and liquid oxygen storage tanks would also be housed in the bunker. Hitler enthusiastically supported the plan, pointing to the success of the massive U-boat shelters constructed on the French coast that had proven to be impervious to British bomber attack.

Surveys of potential sites in the Pas-de-Calais area began in December 1942 and concentrated on the Watten area, due to its proximity to London. The first missile bunker was given the cover-name KNW (Kraftwerk Nordwest: Northwest Electrical Works). Besides the launch bunker in Watten, the nearby town of Wizernes was selected as the location for the main supply base, codenamed SNW (Schotterwerk Nordwest: Northwest Gravel Works). The limestone quarry in the town could be converted into a missile storage site by excavating an extensive network of tunnels. Hitler approved the plan on March 29, 1943 and the KNW bunker was scheduled to be combat-ready by December 31, 1943.

OPPOSITE V-WEAPON SITES: JUNE 1944

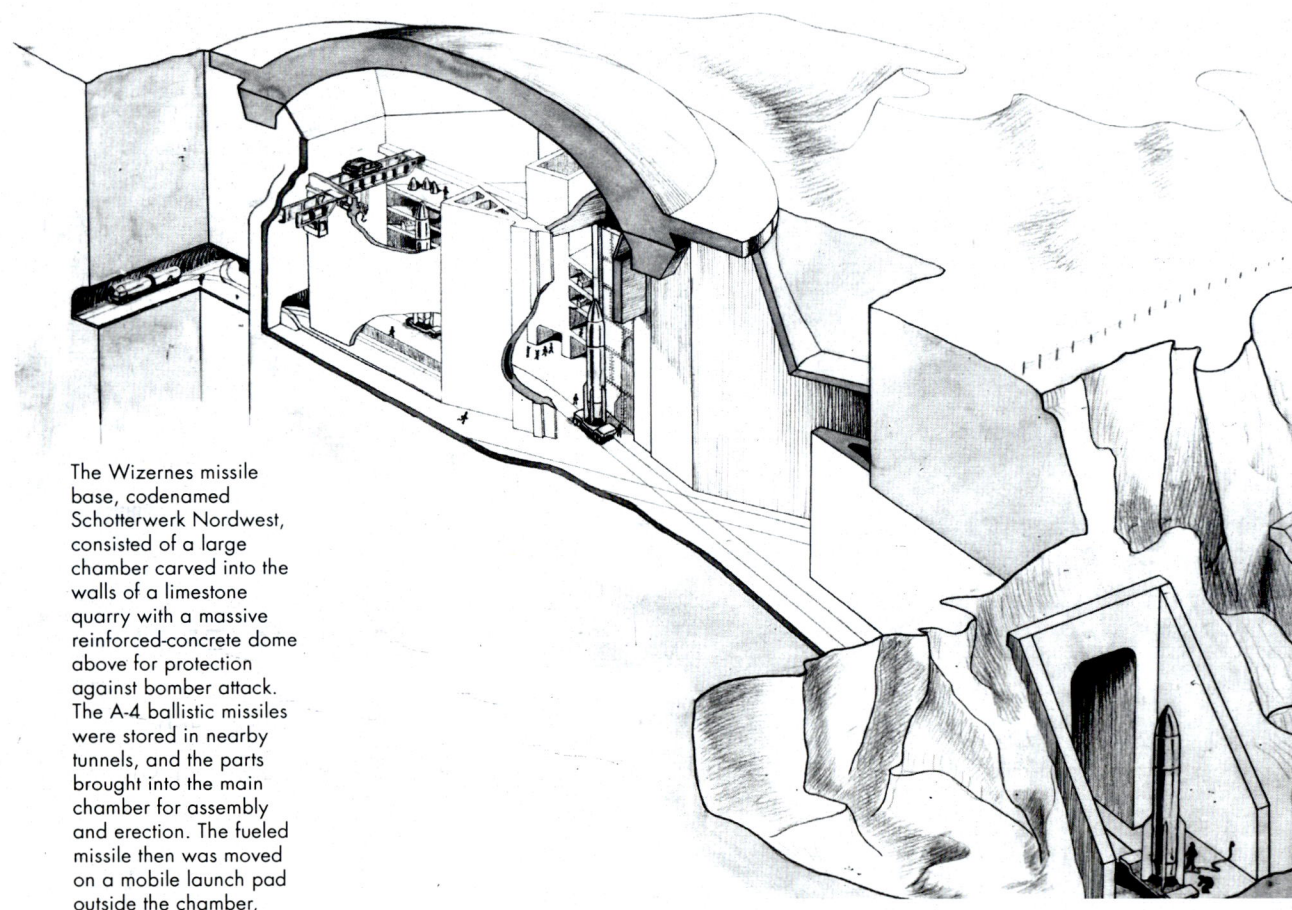

The Wizernes missile base, codenamed Schotterwerk Nordwest, consisted of a large chamber carved into the walls of a limestone quarry with a massive reinforced-concrete dome above for protection against bomber attack. The A-4 ballistic missiles were stored in nearby tunnels, and the parts brought into the main chamber for assembly and erection. The fueled missile then was moved on a mobile launch pad outside the chamber, where it would be launched against London. This is a wartime intelligence drawing of the site, prepared after it was captured in the summer of 1944.

In August 1943, Hitler authorized the construction of an HDP battery in France to supplement the missile campaign against London. Due to the gun's length of 127 meters (417ft), it could not be made mobile and it would inevitably have to be deployed from a fixed site with the barrels inclined at a fixed angle. The most obvious solution was to place it in an underground fortification using inclined tunnels. A site was selected at a limestone hill near Mimoyecques on the Pas-de-Calais. Codenamed Wiese (meadow), initial excavation work for the support tunnels began in late May 1943, even before the gun concept had been fully proven. The initial configuration consisted of two gun batteries, each with five drifts 130 meters (427ft) long, which could each accommodate five HDP barrels for a total of 50 guns. Artillerie Abteilung 705 was organized in January 1944 under Oberstleutnant Georg Borttscheller to operate the Meadow gun complex.

The Luftwaffe's FZG.76 cruise missile was the last of the V-weapons to receive formal deployment approval. Since it was powered by an inexpensive pulse-jet engine, the FZG.76 required a launch ramp long enough for the missile to reach sufficient speed for the motor to operate properly. The method selected was to use a steam catapult system. A gas generator dolly was attached to the base of the launch ramp. To launch the missile, the generator mixed a chemical combination of T-Stoff (hydrogen peroxide) and Z-Stoff (sodium permanganate) to create high-pressure steam that was pumped into a tube inside the launch rail box. This propelled a piston connected underneath the missile, which accelerated it to a speed of about

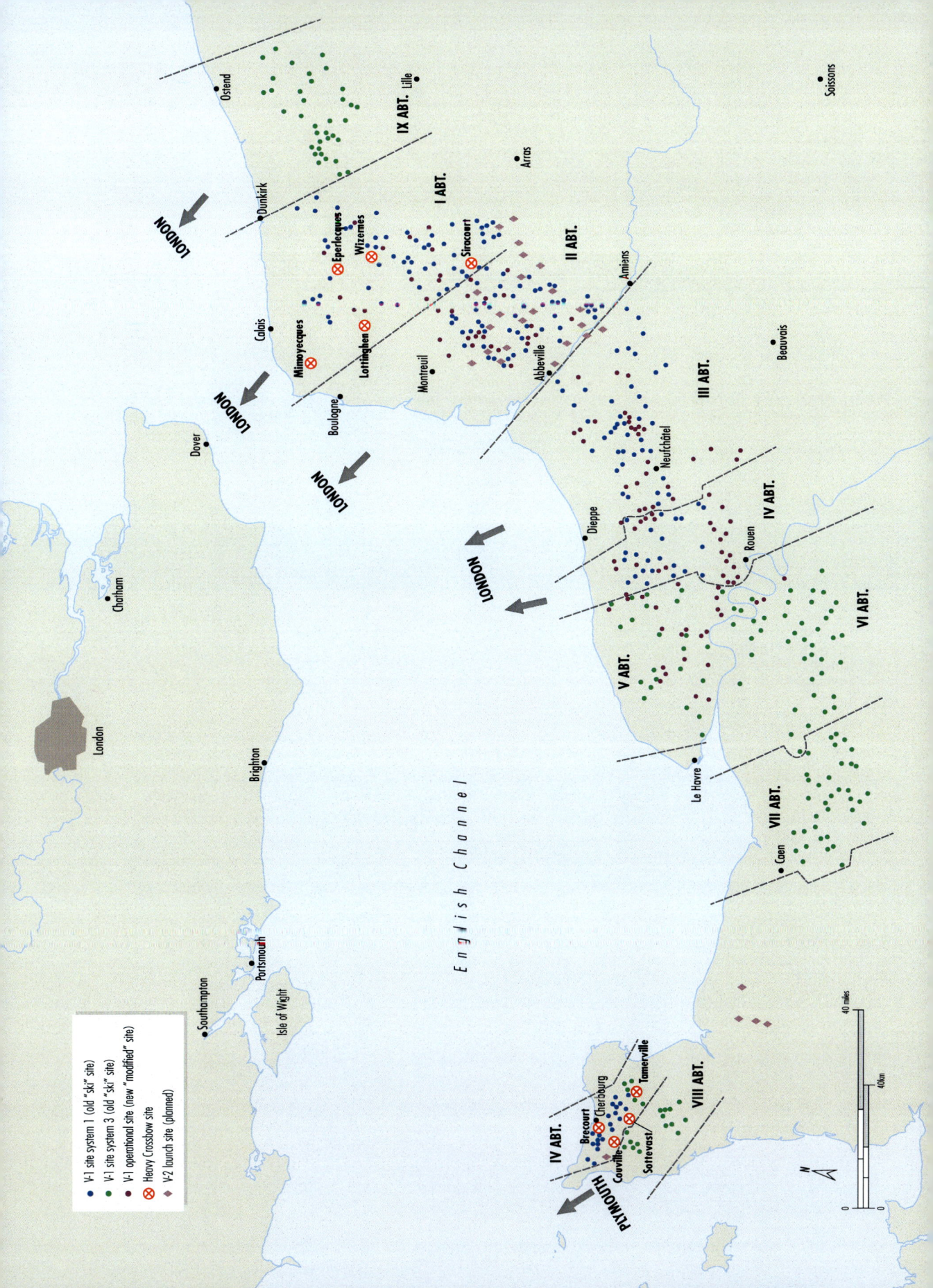

24 DEFENDERS' CAPABILITIES

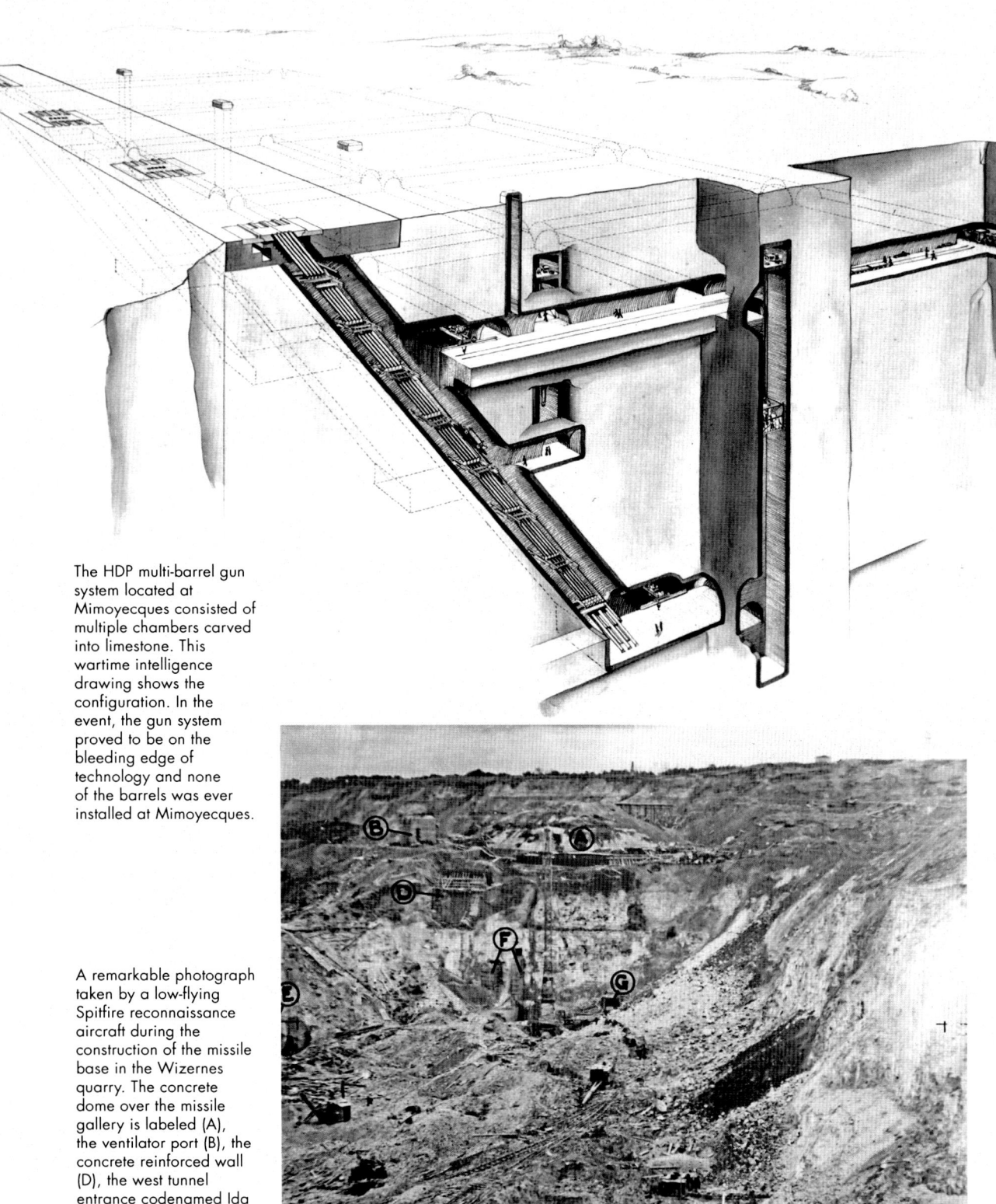

The HDP multi-barrel gun system located at Mimoyecques consisted of multiple chambers carved into limestone. This wartime intelligence drawing shows the configuration. In the event, the gun system proved to be on the bleeding edge of technology and none of the barrels was ever installed at Mimoyecques.

A remarkable photograph taken by a low-flying Spitfire reconnaissance aircraft during the construction of the missile base in the Wizernes quarry. The concrete dome over the missile gallery is labeled (A), the ventilator port (B), the concrete reinforced wall (D), the west tunnel entrance codenamed Ida (E), the east tunnel entrance codenamed Gretchen (F), and the entrance to the original pilot tunnel (G).

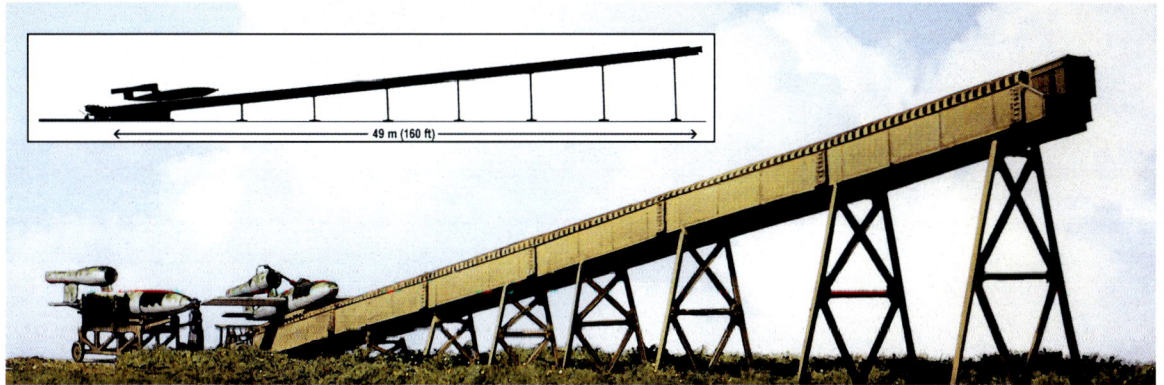

360 meters per second (250mph) by the time it reached the end of the ramp. The launch ramp could be fired and reloaded in 20-minute intervals so it could launch 72 missiles per day at its maximum rate. This was not entirely realistic since each site had accommodation for only 21 missiles, so a more realistic rate-of-fire per launch ramp was about 20 per day.

There was a strenuous debate within the Luftwaffe over fixed versus mobile basing. The Luftwaffe's Flak branch was assigned responsibility for the launch sites, and the Flak commander, Generalleutnant Walther von Axthelm, wanted the missiles deployed in a large number of small "light" launch sites which could be easily camouflaged. However, the head of the Luftwaffe production program, Generalfeldmarschall Erhard Milch, knew that Hitler favored large launch bunkers, so he argued for this approach. A compromise was finally worked out during a meeting with the head of the Luftwaffe, Hermann Göring, on June 18, 1943, with a plan to create four heavy Wasserwerke (waterworks) launch bunkers along with 96 light installations.

The first of the heavy FZG.76 bunker sites were Wasserwerk Desvres located near Lottinghen and Wasserwerk Saint Pol located near Siracourt, both in the Artois region of northeastern France. Another two would follow on the Cotentin Peninsula in lower Normandy, Wasserwerk Valognes near Tamerville, and Wasserwerk Cherbourg at Couville, southeast of the port city. The eventual goal was ten waterworks. Even though this program started several months later than the A-4 launch bunkers, the plan was to have the four waterworks operational at the end of December 1943 to start the missile campaign against London, plus four additional bunkers by March 1944.

Construction of the light launch sites began in the fall of 1943 in the Pas-de-Calais area and near Cherbourg on the Cotentin Peninsula. The initial phase of the program consisted of 64 launch sites and 32 reserve sites. The reserve sites were intended to serve as decoys, but they could be modified for use as operational sites if the need arose. The sites followed a standardized pattern with about a dozen structures including a concrete base for the launch ramp, a launch bunker, a non-magnetic alignment building for the missile guidance system, three missile storage buildings, and several other support buildings for assembling, preparing, and fueling the missiles. The work was supervised by the paramilitary construction firm Organization Todt (OT) but most of the actual work was carried out by local French construction firms. This would prove to be a significant security problem since information about the sites was provided to the French resistance, and in turn, to British intelligence.

To operate the FZG.76 launchers, Flak-Regiment.155W was created on August 1, 1943 under Oberst Max Wachtel at Zempin, about 12 miles (20km) down the coast from Peenemünde. This consisted of four launcher battalions, each having three launch batteries, each with three launch sections, each manning two launch sites for a total of 18 launchers per battalion and 72 launchers in the regiment. The regiment began deploying to France in

The FZG.76 was launched from a Walter Rohrschleuder 2.3t steam catapult ramp. This was built from eight modular sections, each 20 feet (6m) long. A cylinder running the length of the launch ramp contained a piston that was attached to a shoe under the missile. The piston was propelled up the ramp by a gas generator located at the base of the launcher.

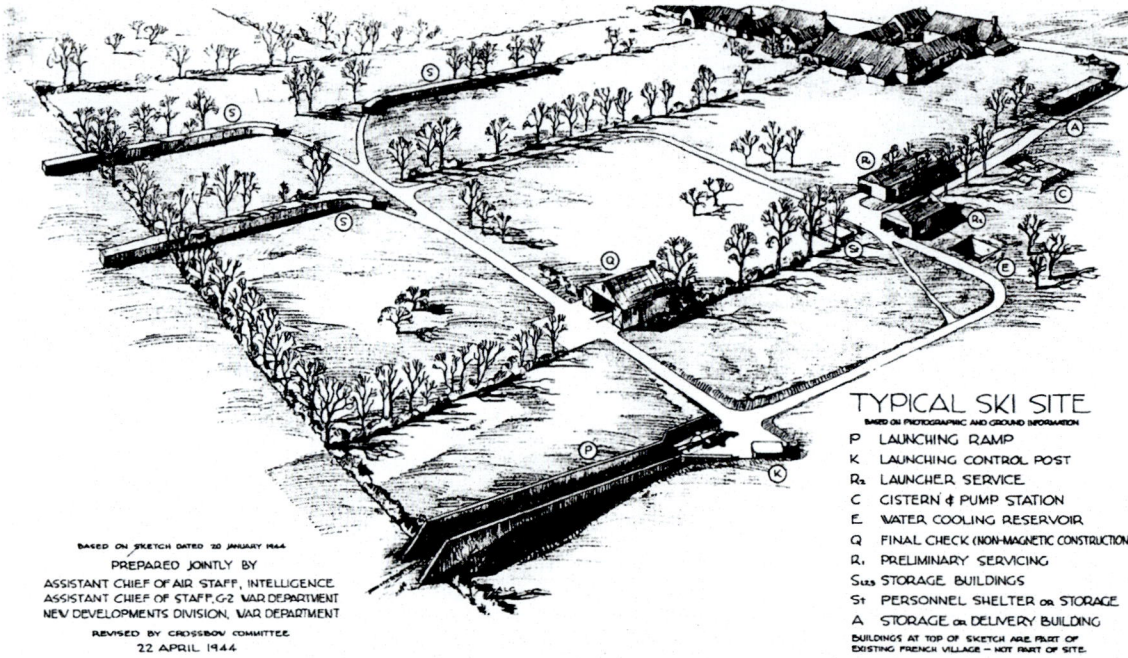

ABOVE This was a widely circulated illustration prepared by the *Crossbow* committee to explain the typical layout of a ski site for photo interpreters. Each of the standard buildings received a letter as seen here that was then used when marking new reconnaissance photos. This illustration was based on the ski site at Maisoncelles, to the east of Le Touquet on the Pas-de-Calais.

RIGHT This is one of the reconnaissance photos of the ski site at Maisoncelles that served as the basis for the well-known *Crossbow* illustration. It was first called Site 77, and was part of the network of sites of the I.Abteilung/FR.155W. The Allied designation for the site was Noball XI/A/55. This photo was taken in late 1943 before the site was completed and, as can be seen, the site is lacking the blast walls usually found on either side of the launcher rail. This particular site was hit 11 times by Allied bombing raids.

mid-October 1943 on the assumption that Operation *Eisbär* would begin on December 1, 1943. The regiment numbered about 6,500 troops and there were a further 4,000 Luftwaffe troops from the 10.Flieger-Division assigned to the program including associated guard, air defense, and transportation units.

In order to coordinate the Heer and Luftwaffe missile programs, the Oberkommando der Wehrmacht (OKW: Armed Forces High Command) established the 65.Armee Korps zur besonderen Verwendung (65th Army Corps for Special Employment) on December 1,

ABOVE The Walter Rohrschleuder 2.3 catapult launcher used a gas generator seen mounted here on a small dolly at the rear of the launcher. When T-Stoff and Z-Stoff were injected into the generator chamber, they produced an impulse of steam that was fed into a cylindrical chamber inside the launch rail, propelling a piston forward. The piston can be seen here in front of the launcher. The piston was connected to a shoe fixed to the underside of the FZG.76, propelling the missile forward.

LEFT This is a partial Walter Rohrschleuder 2.3 catapult launcher preserved at the Val Ygot d'Ardouval museum on the Pas-de-Calais. The launch piston can be seen here on top of the launch rail. The piston is fitted into the cylindrical chamber inside the ramp, with the opening visible at the rear of the launcher.

A US Navy bombardment survey team inspects a Vorratslager storage bunker at one of the sites near Cherbourg in late June 1944. These bunkers could store seven unassembled FZG.76 missiles. Their shape, with a slight curve near the front, led to the Allied nickname "ski site" for the early version of the missile bases.

1943 under the command of Generalleutnant Erich Heinemann, previous commander of the army artillery school. Heinemann immediately began a series of inspection tours of the FZG.76 launch sites, and was dismayed to find that construction was far from complete and that FR.155W was not ready to begin Operation *Eisbär* on schedule. The A-4 ballistic missile program was substantially delayed and had not yet entered serial production and the HDP gun system was likewise months away from operational use. The 65.Armee headquarters sent a detailed report to Berlin on December 24, 1943, making it clear that the missile offensive would be delayed.

Flak-Regiment.155W had a modest organic light flak element consisting of 20mm and 37mm guns intended for site defense against low-altitude aircraft. Little attention was paid to this issue during the original planning on the assumption that "stealth" was the best protection since the ski sites would not be identified. In the event, the Flak units associated with FR.155W proved completely inadequate, owing to the enormous dispersion of the launch sites and the limited capabilities of the 20mm and 37mm automatic Flak cannon when dealing with bombers operating at medium and high altitudes. Wachtel attempted to obtain more defenses for the sites, and some sites, especially the "Heavy Crossbow" sites did receive additional Flak guns in late 1943 and early 1944 as local Luftwaffe resources permitted. There was no dedicated fighter protection for the sites. Allied aircraft losses during Operation *Crossbow* tended to occur due to contact with the overall German air defense network in France and Belgium rather than defenses specific to the Crossbow sites.

LUFTWAFFE ORDER OF BATTLE FOR OPERATION *EISBÄR*, JUNE 1944		
Flak-Regiment.155W (Werfer)		
Unit	Codename (to Aug 1944)	Commanders
FR.155W HQ	Flakgruppe Creil	Oberst Max Wachtel
I Abteilung	Zylinder (Top-hat)	Major Hans Aue
II Abteilung	Werwolf (Werewolf)	Hptm. Rudolf Sack
III Abteilung	Zwieback (Biscuit)	Oberst Lt. Erich Dittrich
IV Abteilung	Zechine (Sequin)	Hptm. Georg Schindler
Signals Abteilung	Vandale (Vandal)	Hptm. Henry Neubert

CAMPAIGN OBJECTIVES
Protecting the capital

Since Operation *Eisbär* was aimed primarily against London, British government and military officials took the initiative in addressing the threat of missile attack. The initial plans focused on preemptive defense. There was some skepticism about the nature and importance of the Heavy Crossbow bunkers and ski sites and no definitive evidence about the capabilities of these missile bases. Nevertheless, British leaders were insistent that the threat be addressed by bombing attacks against the missile bases as well as against potential missile manufacturing sites. Other forms of defensive action against the missile threat, including antiaircraft gun and fighter defenses, did not take shape until the technical details of the V-1 threat became clear in June 1944 after the attacks began.

Despite the substantial Allied air fleets, there was considerable controversy over which elements of these forces would be employed in Operation *Crossbow*. RAF Air Chief Marshal Harris was adamantly opposed to the use of Bomber Command against the missile sites, arguing that they did not have the capability of precision attacks against sites at night and that such missions were better suited to the capabilities of the other elements of Allied air power. He insisted that Bomber Command remain focused on its primary mission of the Combined Bomber Offensive. He eventually relented in his opposition, agreeing to the diversion of some bomber squadrons equipped with the older Stirling bomber since this aircraft was no longer ideal for missions into Germany compared to the preferred Halifax and Lancaster bombers. In addition, Harris agreed to the use of 617 Squadron, the specialized Lancaster squadron that had carried out the Ruhr dam raid. As a result, RAF Bomber Command played a marginal role in the first phase of Operation *Crossbow*.

Harris's views were largely echoed by Gen. Spaatz and the other American heavy bomber commanders. Spaatz was deeply committed to the objectives of Operation *Pointblank* in smashing the Luftwaffe prior to D-Day, and felt that Operation *Crossbow* was a needless diversion of resources. However, Spaatz was less able to argue that the Eighth Air Force was unsuited to precision raids on the Crossbow sites since American bombing doctrine was

Air Chief Marshal Harris refused to commit Bomber Command to Crossbow *missions in 1943 except for the use of Stirling bombers, no longer deemed effective for missions into Germany.*

based on the premise of precision daylight bombing. Furthermore, Eisenhower came under considerable political pressure from Churchill and the British chiefs of staff to employ the Eighth Air Force against the Crossbow sites, and in turn he directed Spaatz to take part in Operation *Crossbow* in spite of his objections. Eisenhower's one concession to Spaatz was to minimize the impact of Operation *Crossbow* on Operation *Pointblank* by using the Eighth Air Force on days when weather precluded missions into Germany. The controversy over the diversion of the Eighth Air Force on *Crossbow* missions continued through 1944 as will be described in detail later.

There was far less controversy over the use of the RAF's 2nd Tactical Air Force or the US 9th Air Force in Operation *Crossbow*. Both of the tactical air forces were primarily intended to provide close-air support of their respective ground forces. In late 1943, this mission was only beginning to take shape in the form of pre-invasion air strikes against targets in France, making them available for *Crossbow* missions.

The objectives for Operation *Crossbow* shifted as more intelligence became available. In the summer of 1943, the problem seemed easily contained since there were only a handful of Heavy Crossbow bunkers identified. Missions against these sites began on August 27, 1943 with the first bomber attack against Watten. The situation changed in the fall of 1943 due to the proliferation of ski sites. On December 2, 1943, the CIU at Medmenham delivered the first comprehensive report on the ski sites to the Air Ministry in London. A fresh round of photographic reconnaissance sorties over France was ordered to make certain that no sites had been missed, and the first orders were issued to begin a comprehensive bombing campaign against the ski sites. Since *Crossbow* was still considered secret, the Crossbow targets were given the codename Noball (also NOBALL, No Ball, etc.). Like the original Bodyline codename, this came from cricket terminology.

The "bomber barons" including Harris, Spaatz, and Doolittle, thought that the area bombardment of the Crossbow sites was needlessly wasteful of bomber missions better directed elsewhere. This is an overhead reconnaissance photo of the area around the Siracourt Heavy Crossbow site, evident in the upper right.

THE CAMPAIGN
Vengence and retaliation

Attacks against the Heavy Crossbow sites began with the August 27, 1943 attack on Watten by the Eighth Air Force. This was followed by smaller attacks on August 30 and September 7. The Mimoyecques site was bombed twice in November by the 2nd Tactical Air Force (2 TAF). The Wasserwerk Cherbourg B8 in Martinvast was hit by a series of small raids between November 25 and December 6, 1943 that delayed construction by several weeks. The bombing attacks were accompanied by leaflet drops that warned French workers that more attacks would follow and that they should abandon their work. The FR.155W war diary mentioned, "The number of French workers is diminishing because of the continual air raids. Even the system of bonuses for increased production is no longer attracting them."

The first wave of *Crossbow* attacks against Noball ski sites began on December 5, 1943 by the Ninth Air Force. Conducted under poor weather conditions, the strikes were ineffective and are not even mentioned in the FR.155W war diary. The 2nd Tactical Air Force also attempted to conduct attacks on the Noball sites but, as in the American case, the overcast weather made effective strikes difficult. These attacks continued through the month. The first strikes to merit any mention in the FR.155W war diary took place on December 14, when three ski sites in the II./FR.155W sector were hit without causing significant damage.

RAF Bomber Command conducted two missions on the night of December 16 to determine the suitability of existing night tactics. Two sites of the II./FR.155W southeast of Abbeville were targeted. The ski site near Flixecourt was marked by six Mosquitoes of 109 Squadron followed by nine Lancasters of 617 Squadron. The marking mission went badly, with the Target Indicators about 350 yards from the site. The second mission against Ailly-le-Haut-Clocher involved six Mosquitoes followed by 26 Stirlings of 75 Squadron. Later RAF assessments concluded that damage to the ski site was negligible but the FR.155W war diary indicates that the Stirlings landed two of their 424 bombs directly on the site and nine nearby, causing some damage.

A line-up of Typhoon fighter bombers of 193 Squadron during a presentation ceremony at Harrowbeer on October 16, 1943. A group of British ex-pats in Brazil made donations to purchase aircraft for the RAF, and funded 15 Typhoons. The aircraft in the foreground carries the name "Bellows of Brazil," named after the group. This squadron began attacks on Noball sites starting the next month.

The unimpressive results from the first attacks prompted the British Air Ministry to remind the British squadrons that *Crossbow* required "maximum concentrated effort" and "overriding priority." On December 15, the British chiefs of staff agreed that the most effective means of attacking the ski sites would be a large-scale daylight operation by the Eighth Air Force. Rather than conduct a series of small raids, a more elaborate scheme called Plan Eye-Que was devised using a massive attack by US medium and heavy bombers along with British medium bombers of the 2 TAF. Mission No. 164 was conducted on December 24, 1943 involving all three bomber divisions of the Eighth Air Force including 722 B-17 and B-24 bombers along with 541 P-47 and P-51 escort fighters of the VIII Fighter Command. The strikes started in the early afternoon against 23 Noball targets, delivering 1,745 tons of bombs. In addition, 221 B-26 bombers of the Ninth Air Force attacked Noball sites that day. The British contribution to Eye-Que was 48 medium bombers of the 2 TAF and 456 Spitfires for escort. This was the largest single mission of the European air war to date. According to German records, only two ski sites were destroyed and three others damaged; casualties were 13 dead and 15 wounded. Allied interpretation of the results was more ambiguous, claiming direct hits on key structures at 11 sites, hits within six other sites, and no hits within five sites. The massive Eye-Que mission showed clearly that the ski sites were not simple targets to destroy using conventional tactics.

By year's end, Allied units had bombed 52 Noball sites with 12 sustaining Category A damage; nine Category B, 15 Category C, and ten sites Category D. These assessments were based on aerial photographs. Category A meant that there had been a concentration of impacts within the ski site with direct hits against one or more critical buildings. Category B meant that there had been hits within the site with impacts close enough to damage key buildings. Category C meant that there had been impacts within the site, and Category D meant that there had been no impacts within the site. German records indicate that "seven have been destroyed, three of them having been obliterated."

British officials had been reluctant to explain their intelligence concerns to their American counterparts in any detail until mid-December due to the high level of uncertainty. There was a flurry of joint meetings to clarify the situation in order to win full American support for an expanded countermeasures campaign. As a result, the US War Department set up its own *Crossbow* committee on December 29 to supplement the British *Crossbow* subcommittee of the JIC. General George C. Marshall, the head of the US Joint Chiefs of Staff warned Field Marshal Sir John Dill, Britain's highest ranking British official in Washington, that "we cannot lend fullest support to this project, particularly in the field of countermeasures, unless we have full information on the British progress in meeting this problem." There was some concern in Washington that the Crossbow sites might pose a threat to Operation *Overlord* due to the sites around Cherbourg aimed at Portsmouth. The most alarming assessment by Army Air Forces Headquarters suggested that the attacks could involve biological warfare, chemical warfare, and the use of revolutionary explosives of "unusually violent character," a hint of American concern over the German quest for an atomic bomb.

The Eglin Field trials

After reviewing the information provided by the RAF, Gen. Henry H. "Hap" Arnold, head of the USAAF, concluded that RAF assessments of damage to the Noball sites were based on "guesswork and speculation." He wished to determine what types of air attack on the ski sites would bring the best results and, on January 13, 1944, the *Crossbow* committee of the US War Department recommended a "technical and tactical inquiry into the means, methods and effectiveness of air attacks on Crossbow targets in France." On January 25, Arnold instructed Brig. Gen. Grandison Gardiner, commander of the AAF Proving Ground at Eglin Field in Florida, to construct a replica of a ski site, and then subject it to a variety

This is Target C, a full-scale replica of a German FZG.76 ski site, created at the Eglin Proving Ground in Florida in January 1944 to test bombing tactics. The ski-shaped storage buildings are evident on the right.

of attacks to determine which tactics were most effective in destroying these missile bases. He stressed to Gardiner that he wanted the project completed in "days, not weeks." A contractor began work at the selected site the next day, based on plans from the CIU at Medmenham. The six targets were created in 12 days using 5,085 cubic yards of concrete, 44,000 concrete blocks, 21,000 bricks, 120 tons of steel re-bar, and 40,000 feet of lumber. Each target contained at least two of the most critical structures identified by the RAF. Targets A and B were dummies used for original target orientation and not intended for actual attack. The structures were completed by February 7 but the first concrete structures were not available for test until February 11 in order to let the concrete cure. Aircraft and crews were provided by the 9th Bomb Group and 50th Fighter Group. To provide greater realism, several of the sites were defended by antiaircraft guns.

The Eglin tests were conducted in four phases: identification and accuracy; practice in tactical methods; effectiveness of munitions; and operational tests. The initial identification and accuracy Phase I involved medium bombers and heavy bombers attacking from medium altitude (12,000ft) and high altitude (20,000ft) using conventional bombs as well as guided bombs. The light bomber (B-25 with 75mm gun) and fighter tests were conducted at minimum altitude or using glide attack. Besides the use of camouflage nets at some of the targets, smokescreens were also tested.

Phase II was intended to determine the optimum number of aircraft needed to destroy a ski site including fighter and bomber types. Phase III was intended to examine the effectiveness of various munitions including unguided and guided 500lb and 1,000lb general purpose (GP) and semi-armor-piercing (SAP) bombs; incendiary bombs; aircraft rockets; oil spray from fighters; and assorted special bombs including pre-set glide bombs and radio-guided

AZON bombs. Some of these weapons were under consideration as a means to burn away camouflage netting commonly used at the Noball sites.

Phase IV was intended to determine the best balance using a minimum number of aircraft types to destroy a single Noball site. The first series of tests were conducted on February 10–24, 1944 and the report released on March 1.

The initial tests concluded that high-speed, low-altitude aircraft were the most effective and least vulnerable to enemy antiaircraft fire. It was also found that coordinated attacks from different directions increased aircraft survivability and the probability of hitting the targets. The B-26 medium bomber was found to have a 30 percent hit rate using 1,000lb GP and 2,000lb GP bombs at minimum altitude while P-38 and P-47 fighters using the same weapons had hit rates of 18 percent at minimum altitude and 12 percent in glide attacks. High-altitude B-17 attacks using the 500lb GP bomb, the tactic favored by the British Air Ministry, had the poorest results with only a 2.1 percent hit rate. Some weapons including rockets and guided bombs gave surprisingly poor results. The B-25 with 75mm cannon demonstrated a high percentage of target hits but there was some uncertainty over its effectiveness because there was little knowledge of the contents of the ski site buildings and the fragmentation inside the test buildings was modest. A second series of tests were conducted in March 1944, mainly to test other munitions including white phosphorus bombs.

At the conclusion of the first set of trials, Gen. Gardiner headed a mission to Britain to brief US and British officials. The senior American officials including Arnold, Spaatz, Brereton, and Vandenberg felt that the Eglin tests validated their belief that high-altitude attack using heavy bombers was wasteful, and they wished to see the effort shift to the medium bombers and fighter bombers of the Ninth Air Force. The RAF, however, remained committed to the use of heavy bombers against both ski sites and Heavy Crossbow sites. Air Chief Marshal Trafford Leigh-Mallory, head of the new AEAF (Allied Expeditionary Air Force), and the principal RAF commander concerned with *Crossbow*, wrote to Spaatz on March 4 after the Eglin briefing that "I think it is clear now that the best weapon for the rocket sites is the high altitude bomber." Some British officers were skeptical about the Eglin tests, arguing that the test buildings were better protected than the actual German buildings even though the test site was constructed using information from the CIU at Medmenham. Other RAF officers contended that low-altitude attacks were likely to be too costly due to the increasing amount of Flak positions appearing in the Pas-de-Calais and Cherbourg areas. A postwar US Air Force history suggested that the RAF's refusal to try the Eglin tactics was triggered by the personality clash between Spaatz and Leigh-Mallory, and Leigh-Mallory's notorious stubbornness in the face of dissent against his views. The controversy over this issue poisoned relations between the senior US commanders, Leigh-Mallory's AEAF headquarters, and the British Air Ministry. It would have repercussions later in the summer when Operation *Eisbär* was finally started.

Polar Bear's new bases

After Gen. Heinemann's 65.Korps headquarters was established near Saint-Germain in December 1943, Heinemann and his staff began a tour of the missile bases in France and Belgium. Heinemann was an experienced artillery commander and was well aware of the risk of counter-battery fire. From his perspective, the FZG.76 light sites were too conspicuous, too time-consuming to construct, and too vulnerable. On December 24, 1943, the OKW sent his headquarters a teletype indicating that Berlin expected Operation *Eisbär* to commence on January 1, 1944. Heinemann quickly realized that Berlin had no real appreciation of the many delays in the construction of the launch sites, the training of the crews, or the delivery of the actual missiles. He held a series of meetings with key officials in France and Germany to assess the likely pace of site construction as well as the delivery schedule for the new missiles. On January 5, 1944, he completed a report personally addressed to Hitler that indicated that Operation *Eisbär* should concentrate on the FZG.76 since the A-4 ballistic missile was still so severely delayed that there were no accurate forecasts for its initial operational use. He estimated that the FZG.76 might be ready for combat use in four or five months. Heinemann insisted that 65.Korps take over control of the missile base construction and that, for security reasons, the French construction firms be replaced by German firms using military construction units. He also recommended that the current configuration of FZG.76 light sites be abandoned in favor of simplified sites that could be constructed much more rapidly and which could be used in field conditions under the threat of Allied air attack. Heinemann presented the report to Generalfeldmarschall Wilhelm Keitel, OKW chief of staff, at the 15.Armee headquarters in Tourcoing on January 10, 1944. Heinemann's executive officer, Oberst Eugen Walter, later wrote that Hitler probably never saw the report, presumably due to its frank assessment of Hitler's pet project and the bad light it cast on many senior German officials.

Opposition to Heinemann's plan came mainly from Organization Todt (OT) which, as a matter of professional pride, wished to prove that its concrete structures could withstand a bombing campaign. As the intensity of Allied bombing attacks continued through early 1944, the OT's boasts became increasingly hollow. Heinemann also managed to weaken the opposition from OT by diverting their attention to the construction of bomb-proof tunnels and bunkers for missile storage that were essential in the conduct of any prolonged missile campaign. Hitler was gradually informed of the delays in the program as well as Heinemann's proposal to shift to a more flexible basing for the FZG.76. He agreed with the proposal, but instructed that some work should be continued on the existing missile bases to divert Allied bombs from the new missile sites.

As a result of the change in plan, the network of "Old Pattern Sites" (SaB: Stellungen alter Bauart) was designated at Stellung-System.I while the new network of "Operational Sites" (EiS: Einsatz Stellungen) was designated as Stellung-System.II. Construction of the new sites began in late February 1944. The new firing sites were configured with an absolute minimum of permanent structures. The new configuration retained the same catapult launch rail system, but without the distinctive blast walls on either side. The catapult ramps took about seven or eight days to erect, and were brought to a site only at the start of the

During the spring of 1944, Allied intelligence found it nearly impossible to locate the new modified sites. This photo explains why. Until the launch rails were moved into place, the modified site consisted of little more than some small concrete base plates along with rails for the overhead crane to install the launcher. These were covered with sod or other camouflage as seen at a site near Cherbourg, making them virtually impossible to see from overhead photographic reconnaissance.

The basic assemblies of the FZG.76 missile were delivered to a Luftwaffen Zeugamt (assembly point) in western Germany where they were mounted on a transport dolly for shipment to the forward supply centers in France. This example at the depot at Dannenberg is nearly complete except for the wings, which were placed on either side of the fuselage for shipment. The warhead was not fitted to the missile until final assembly at the launch site, and the bucket at the front of the missile contains the fuzes and other delicate sub-assemblies.

missile campaign. Basic pilings for the launch ramp, a flat platform for the steam generator trolley, and a foundation for the non-magnetic guidance shed were made from concrete. The new sites were generally positioned near French farms where the existing buildings could be used for crew accommodations and storage. Certain of the specialized buildings such as the navigation correction building used prefabricated wooden sheds instead of concrete structures. The distinctive ski buildings were not used and missiles were either stored in available buildings or left under camouflage nets. When time permitted, some small structures were built, especially the steam generator preparation shed, workshops for preparing the missile, fuel storage sheds, and the launch bunker near the catapult, and, in some cases, prefabricated structures were used.

It took a work party of 40 men only about two weeks to construct such a site; the original ski sites had taken three to four months with a much larger construction crew. In addition, the sites were prepared for construction, but the launch rail and other obvious structures were not erected at the sites, until Operation *Eisbär* was ready to start. None of these buildings was especially conspicuous, and the new sites proved to be almost invisible to air detection until the launch ramps began to be erected in June 1944. By the middle of March 1944, 32 new sites had been prepared. In total, the Stellung-System.II included five launch sites per launch battery plus a support site, for a total of 80 launch sites and 16 support sites. To reduce the vulnerability of Stellung-System.II to Allied intelligence, the work was undertaken only by German military construction crews and French workers were barred from the site.

In the spring of 1944, work began on Stellung-System.III, a new series of launch sites in the Cherbourg area and southwest of the River Seine that would be manned by a proposed second regiment, FR.255W. As a result, IV./FR.155W was moved back from the Cherbourg area to take up new positions near the regiment's other three battalions in northeastern France.

The missile supply network

The ability of FR.155W to launch a continual stream of missiles depended on a robust supply system. Since this later became a major focus of the Allied bombing attacks, it is worth describing in some detail. This network consisted of three main layers. The FZG.76 was not delivered as a complete aircraft from the factories. Rather, its major subcomponents were shipped to a Luftwaffen Zeugamt (assembly point) in western Germany. The most important of these were Pulverhof in Mecklenberg and Karlwitz near Dannenberg. These assembly points collected the main subcomponents from various factories, and then loaded the components for a single FZG.76, minus the warhead, on a storage pallet (Doppelpallung) or the similar, wheeled transport dolly (TW-76 Abstellpallung) for shipment to the front. The warheads were prepared at a Luft-Munas (Luftwaffen Munitionsanstalt; munitions plant) for separate shipment for safety reasons, as was the fuel.

The assembly points then shipped the missile pallets by rail to depots in France. The Luftwaffe planned to create more than a dozen of these depots for Operation *Eisbär*, though not all were ready when the missile campaign started. These had a variety of configurations. Several used natural caves or tunnel systems, while others used newly constructed concrete warehouses. The three most important at the outset of the campaign were: Leopold near Saint-Leu-d'Esserent, Nordpol near Nucourt, and Richard near Rilly-la-Montagne.

FZG.76 FORWARD DEPOTS		
Codename	Location	Missile capacity
Leopold	Saint-Leu-d'Esserent	1,600–2,400
Nordpol	Nucourt	1,000–1,500
Richard	Rilly-la-Montagne	1,000–1,500
Karl-Theodor	Ytres Canal Tunnel	1,000–1,500
Bertha	Bessancourt	1,000–1,500
Martha	Saint Maximin/Creil	1,000
Christina	Chanteloup	1,000
Laura	Laigneville	1,000
Murmeltier	Mamers	650
Luchs	Luché	300
Chamäleon	Cherbourg	300
Bieber	Balleau	275
Anton	Fort VII Antwerp	240
Christa	Fort Cruybeke	200
Robert	Fort Rochambeau	150
Hildegard	Fort Hirson	150

The final level for missile supply was much closer to the launch sites, so that they could be conveniently reached by the battalion transport section using trucks rather than railcars. The FZG.76 pallet, warhead, and support equipment were delivered to a Versorgungslager (supply depot), usually with one depot per launch battalion. There was a separate Betriebsstofflager (fuel depot) for the aviation fuel and the steam catapult chemicals. In turn, the launcher battalions would send trucks to pick up new shipments of missiles and fuel which were kept in small local depots not far from the launch batteries.

The Allied interdiction campaign against the railroad network in France and the neighboring countries was a major impediment to supplying missiles to the launch sites. This is a supply train of FZG.76 in their standard shipping configuration with three missile pallets per rail car.

Crossbow Phase I

The *Crossbow* campaign is usually broken down into phases, with Phase I covering the start of the campaign in the fall of 1943 to the start of Operation *Eisbär* in June 1944. During Phase I, the bomber missions were divided between the ski sites and the principal Heavy Crossbow bunkers, as well as some suspected storage sites.

The Eighth Air Force conducted attacks on Noball targets only on days when the weather over Germany was too poor to permit missions. The first large attack of the new year took place on January 14, 1944 involving 552 B-17 and B-24 bombers. This attack introduced the use of delayed fuzes on a portion of the bombs which were set to detonate 18 hours after impact. The intention was to discourage the work crews from repairing the sites. FR.155W reported that 28 sites were damaged by the attack, of which 20 were seriously damaged.

The usual Eighth Air Force pattern for the attacks on the Noball ski sites was to employ large mass attacks, often using all three bomber divisions. Attacks were usually conducted in boxes of six bombers from altitudes of 12,000 to 20,000 feet. Weather had a major impact

on mission success since it was necessary to acquire the target in the Norden bomb sight about 6 miles from the target to ensure good accuracy. From January 1944 through D-Day, the Eighth Air Force launched 13 missions against the ski sites totaling 5,716 bomber sorties and delivering 12,658 tons of bombs. Attacks on the five principal Heavy Crossbow bunkers were conducted mainly by the B-24 bombers of the 2nd Bomb Division. There were a total of 24 missions against the bunkers during this period, involving 1,841 bomber sorties and 5,063 tons of bombs. There was a significant disparity in the volume of bombing directed against the Heavy Crossbow sites, with the heavy sites receiving on average 1,012 tons of bombs while the average ski site received 131 tons from Eighth Air Force bombers.

RAF Bomber Command conducted a small number of raids on Crossbow sites in January 1944. The largest was a raid on the night of January 21/22 against four ski sites starting with Mosquitoes to mark the targets followed by 12 Lancasters, and 89 Stirlings, dropping 451 tons of bombs. There was another raid on the night of January 25/26 involving 37 Stirling and 12 Lancaster bombers. This largely ended Bomber Command participation in *Crossbow* until the summer due to Air Chief Marshal Harris's belief that results to date had been poor owing to the difficulties of attacking such small and indistinct targets at night. Up to this point, Bomber Command conducted 479 *Crossbow* sorties, dropping about 1,850 tons of bombs. Over the next few months, the only significant Bomber Command participation in *Crossbow* was a series of small-scale raids by Mosquitoes against the Heavy Crossbow sites.

The first large-scale attack on the ski sites was conducted on December 24, 1943 by the Eighth Air Force. This is the attack on a ski site of I./FR.155W near the Bois de Crequy near Rimboval on the Pas-de-Calais, designated as Noball site XI/A/82 by Allied intelligence. The raid involved 27 B-17 bombers, mainly of the 100th Bomb Group, and was the first of three to hit the site.

RAF Fighter Command provided escort for many of the *Crossbow* missions. This is a Spitfire IX of the 302 (Polish) Squadron escorting the B-24 bombers of the 2nd Bomb Division on a Noball mission in December 1943.

ABOVE The Boston was flown by several squadrons of the 2nd Tactical Air Force including 107 Squadron seen here. This unit took part in Noball missions through late 1943 and into 1944 before converting to Mosquitoes.

RIGHT Mitchells of the Dutch 320 Squadron joined 2nd Tactical Air Force in the summer of 1943 and are seen here bombing up for a mission from RAF Lasham. The squadron was heavily involved in attacks against Noball sites in late 1943 and early 1944. (Library and Archives Canada, MIKAN 4447459)

Although the Eighth Air Force was responsible for the greatest tonnage delivered against Crossbow targets in Phase I, the two tactical air forces conducted the largest number of sorties. These peaked in January 1944 with about 4,500 sorties that month, declining in subsequent months as more and more missions were committed in support of the pre-invasion phase of Operation *Overlord*. The 2nd Tactical Air Force conducted most of its *Crossbow* missions using Mitchell and Boston bombers from 2 Group. Fighters of the 2nd Tactical Air Force were mainly used for harassment attacks on the ski sites days after the bomber strikes to discourage and disrupt repair work.

The backbone of the Ninth Air Force *Crossbow* missions was the B-26 Marauder equipping two of the bombardment wings, and the A-20 Havoc equipping one wing. The Ninth Air Force scheduled 25 Noball missions in January 1944, but 16 missions failed to engage the target due to overcast winter weather. In total, the Ninth Air Force launched 1,740 sorties in January 1944 of which 1,022 reached the targets and dropped 1,521 tons of bombs. Ninety-three percent of all tactical air force bomber missions in January 1944 were devoted to *Crossbow*, the peak period of participation. The number of missions by the Ninth Air Force and 2nd Tactical Air Force fell to under 2,500 in February, due in large measure to adverse weather, and the diversion of the Ninth Air Force late in the month to support Operation *Argument*, an escalation of the Eighth Air Force's Operation *Pointblank*. The Ninth Air Force conducted about 970 Noball sorties in February 1944, dropping about 1,450 tons of bombs. Attacks on Noball targets by the Ninth Air Force increased in March 1944 due to improving spring weather, with a total of ten missions involving 1,100 sorties against 34 sites with about 1,390 tons of bombs. For the first time, five Ninth Air Force fighter groups conducted dive-bombing missions on Noball sites on March 29. This was not officially sanctioned and subsequent fighter-bomber missions in support of *Crossbow* were directed mainly to the flak suppression mission.

On March 27, Leigh-Mallory's AEAF headquarters took over control of the tactical air forces in order to support Operation *Overlord*. This generally led to a shift away from *Crossbow* assignments and towards other missions. The Ninth Air Force missions received a new emphasis on railway targets and initial strikes on coastal artillery positions of the Atlantic Wall. Crossbow targets had second priority to *Overlord*. In March, a total of 4,250 tons of bombs were dropped in 2,800 sorties. The priority for *Crossbow* missions declined precipitously in May 1944 when the Ninth Air Force and 2nd Tactical Air Force were shifted almost entirely to the support of the forthcoming Normandy invasion.

NEUTRALIZATION OF SKI SITES BY COMMAND (PHASE I: DECEMBER 1943 TO JUNE 1944)	
Eighth Air Force	35
Ninth Air Force	39
2nd Tactical Air Force	33

The single most effective aircraft during Phase I of Operation *Crossbow* was the Mosquito, mainly those of 2 Group. This is a Mosquito B Mk. IV, which had the bulged doors to permit it to carry larger payloads including the 4,000lb "Cookie" Blockbuster bomb.

A Mosquito FB Mk.VI of the 487 Squadron (RNZAF) that served with No. 140 Wing of the 2nd Tactical Air Force. This unit began taking part in *Crossbow* missions in early 1944, including the raid on the Ruisseauville ski site on January 4, 1944.

An assessment by FR.155W on February 25, 1944 concluded:

By 24 February, 392 enemy air missions had been made against the regiment's sites, of which 330 were high altitude and 62 low altitude. Some 7,000 aircraft had dropped 19,000 bombs of various types including delayed action bombs. Some sites have suffered serious damage, but the overall damage is in no way proportionate to the enemy's effort. Nine sites were damaged beyond repair, eight of these in Werewolf (II Abt.) which bore the brunt of the raids. Another 29 sites were seriously damaged, 20 suffered medium damage while 25 of the sites that were attacked went unscathed.

German defenses during Phase I varied through time. German fighter interceptions were significant in late 1943, but largely evaporated by the end of January 1944. This was due to the heavy presence of Allied escort fighters as well as the general recall of fighter units back to Germany to counter Operation *Pointblank*. In the case of flak, there were only about 60 light AA guns and 60 heavy AA guns protecting the Crossbow sites in late 1943, but, by the end of May 1944, this had increased to about 730 light AA guns and 520 heavy AA guns. In addition, the Crossbow sites in the Cherbourg area also saw an increase from about 120 heavy AA guns to 200 by May 1944.

ALLIED ASSESSMENT OF CUMULATIVE BOMB DAMAGE TO SKI SITES					
Category	A	B	C	D	Total attacked*
Dec 31, '43	12	9	15	10	52
Jan 15, '44	17	32	13	9	76
Feb 29, '44	50	27	16	4	97
Apr 1, '44	65	20	11	0	96
May 13, '44	76	14	3	0	96
Jun 11, '44	82	12	2	0	96
* Note: some sites received no damage at all or could not be assessed					

GERMAN ASSESSMENT OF DAMAGE TO LAUNCH SITES			
Date	Dec 31, 1943	Mar 31, 1944	Apr 31, 1944
Totally destroyed	3	9	9
Seriously damaged	7	29	35
Medium damage	–	20	29
Light damage	–	20	20
Intact	–	25	10
Not attacked	–	–	1

A post-strike overhead photo of the Le Sorellerie III ski site after a Noball mission on February 15, 1944 by the Ninth Air Force. The launch ramp area (P), "ski" storage buildings (S), and non-magnetic alignment building (Q) have all suffered significant damage. This ski site was in the Cherbourg area, originally intended for operation by IV./FR.155W.

AIRCRAFT EFFECTIVENESS AGAINST SKI SITES (CATEGORY A DAMAGE)		
Type	Number of Category A strikes	Average Tonnage
B-17	30	195.1
B-24	5	401.4
B-26	26	223.5
B-25	10.5	244.0
A-20	4	313.0
Mosquito	19.5	39.8
Spitfire	3	50.3

A pair of B-17Gs of the 452nd Bomb Group during Mission 280 on March 26, 1944 attacking Noball sites in the Cherbourg area.

Initial attacks on the Heavy Crossbow sites

The Heavy Crossbow sites were small in number but proved the easiest to identify due to their size. They were widely viewed with the most anxiety and were subjected to particularly intense air attack.

As described earlier, the Watten site was the first hit in late August 1943, and it continued to be attacked through 1943 and into 1944. The Watten site was struck with bombs up to 2,000lb in size but these could not penetrate the steel-reinforced concrete roof. Nevertheless, the bombing around the site cratered all the roads and rail lines being used for construction,

ABOVE An A-20G of the 669th Bomb Squadron, 416th Bombardment Group, Ninth Air Force on a mission over France in late April 1944, probably one of the Noball missions over Bois d'Enfer or Bonnieres, France. During the month of April, the group struck Noball targets on 20 of its missions.

RIGHT "Lorelei," a B-26C of the 558th BS, 387th Bomb Group during a mission in May 1944. This aircraft was lost on June 23, 1944 after flying 45 missions.

making it impossible to complete its construction. Although there were still plans to use it to produce liquid oxygen for the A-4 ballistic missile, the plans to use the site were gradually abandoned and some work was continued mainly to encourage the Allied air forces to waste their bombs. From January to June 1944, Watten was hit with eight more heavy-bomber attacks by the Eighth Air Force, dropping over 500 tons of bombs on the site.

The severe damage caused by the initial attack on Watten on August 27, 1943 convinced Organization Todt to shift the construction technique to a new method called "earth forming" (Erdschalung), in which the roof was built on top of an earth mound to prevent its destruction by bombing during construction. Once the roof was complete and the concrete fully cured, the area under the roof was excavated to create the inner chamber of the bunker. Although this technique was reasonably successful in creating bomb-resistant roofs, it could not prevent the desolation of the area around the bunker, which continued to make completion an impossible challenge. The use of this technique was most apparent at the Siracourt site.

As it became increasingly apparent that Watten could never function as an A-4 launch site, the nearby Wizernes limestone quarry site, originally intended for A-4 assembly, was converted into a launch site with an enormous reinforced dome cover over the missile erection chamber. This site began to attract substantial Allied attention in March 1944 and the dome was directly hit at least once on a raid on May 6, 1944 without penetrating the chamber below.

The first major attack on the German missile sites was on August 27, 1943 when 187 B-17 bombers of the 1st and 4th Bombardment Wings attacked the Kraftwerk Nordwest bunker at Watten. Among the units participating in the attack was the 410th BS, 94th Bomb Group, 4th Bombardment Wing. One of its aircraft, B-17F "Virgin's Delight," is seen here. This particular aircraft was shot down by German fighters near Sollingen on November 29, 1943 during a raid on Bremen.

ALLIED SORTIES AGAINST THE HEAVY CROSSBOW SITES JAN–JUNE 1944							
	Jan	Feb	Mar	Apr	May	Jun	Total
Watten	0	469	614	311	345	201	1,940
Wizernes	0	0	450	480	163	953	2,046
Siracourt	189	943	308	538	1,527	1,126	4,631
Lottinghen	0	297	209	99	0	0	605
Mimoyecques	0	0	339	319	284	1,399	2,341
Total	189	1,709	1,920	1,747	2,319	3,679	11,563

The crew of B-17F 42-29754 "Shangri-La Lil" of the 360th BS, 303rd Bombardment Group, piloted by 2Lt. George Crockett, pose in front of their aircraft on August 12, 1943. This aircraft was hit by flak on the first major Eighth Air Force mission against the Heavy Crossbow site at Watten on August 27, 1943. Most of the crew in the nose of the aircraft were killed by the flak burst while five others parachuted to safety and became prisoners of war. Four aircraft were lost on this mission.

The Mimoyecques gun site was hit by B-26 bombers of the Ninth Air Force on November 5, 1943 and twice more in 1943. In the wake of the air attacks, Organization Todt decided to scale back the project by halting work on the western batteries before any shafts were created, and concentrating on the eastern battery. The site was hit again with four more raids by the Eighth Air Force in January–June 1944 totaling a further 450 tons of bombs.

Wasserwerk Cherbourg B8 near Martinvast on the Cotentin Peninsula was heavily damaged by air attack by 162 medium bombers of the Ninth Air Force on November 11, 1943, during the preparatory stages of construction. This bunker did not progress beyond excavation work due to continuing attacks against the site through January 1944. A different fate befell Wasserwerk Valognes B7 at Tamerville on the Cotentin Peninsula. Work was delayed due to a general reconsideration of the prospects for the Waterworks after the November 11 raid on Martinvast. In the meantime, Erwin Rommel stumbled on to the site, while on one of his tours of the Atlantic Wall defenses. The launch site was very close to the command post of the 709.Infanterie Division defending this sector, and so the army commanders pressured Organization Todt to halt construction and divert the resources to the coastal defenses instead. The Tamerville site was downgraded to a reserve site with little substantial construction work.

The Wasserwerk Desvres at Lottinghen was hit for the first time on February 24, 1944, eventually absorbing nine raids and 605 tons of bombs. The attacks undermined the side walls before the roof could be constructed, so in April 1944 construction at the site was abandoned. Wasserwerk Saint Pol near Siracourt was first hit on January 31, 1944 but this bunker was the only one of the original four to nearly reach completion. The reinforced-concrete roof entered construction in the last weeks of March 1944 in spite of repeated attacks; Siracourt was struck a total of 27 times with about 5,000 tons of bombs. By D-Day, concrete work was almost complete but only about half of the excavation had been finished, since it was necessary to dig out the soil under the roof. The plans called for completion of the site by mid-July but the launch ramps were never started and, indeed, the final configuration of the site is something of a mystery.

To make up the shortfall of large launch bunkers, in March 1944, the Luftwaffe decided to reinvigorate construction of the proposed army Ölkeller Cherbourg, a series of tunnels near Brécourt in the Cherbourg suburbs which had been intended for storing A-4 ballistic missiles. The A-4 was not yet ready for production. Instead the tunnels would serve as the preparation and storage area for the FZG.76 missiles, while protected launch ramps were added to turn the facility into a gigantic fortified launch site. This new configuration was called Wasserwerk No. 2 and was expected to be able to contain 300 FZG.76 missiles, enough for about six days of launches. Due to its use of existing French tunnels, the site was never identified as a Crossbow target by Allied intelligence. Most of the main construction was completed in the week after D-Day but the site was captured during the Cherbourg campaign in June 1944 before any missiles were launched.

The August 12, 1943 attack on the Kraftwerk Nordwest bunker near Watten ruined the northern half of the structure. This is a reconnaissance photo taken some time later after the debris has been cleared from the damaged section.

48 THE CAMPAIGN

It was obvious to Allied intelligence analysts that the existing bombs were inadequate to penetrate the thick reinforced concrete roofs of the Heavy Crossbow sites. The RAF had already initiated work on a super-heavy bomb capable of penetrating steel-reinforced concrete because of the requirement to destroy German submarine bunkers on the Atlantic coast. This had been entrusted to Barnes Wallis, the engineer who had developed the Upkeep bouncing bombs, used so successfully in the raids against the Ruhr dams in 1943 by 617 Squadron. The first of these, codenamed Tallboy, entered development in the summer of 1943. It weighed 4,000lb and used a hardened steel nose and rear fuze to permit penetration of the concrete, followed by delayed detonation once the bomb casing had entered into the bunker chamber below. The first tests of the Tallboy took place on April 18, 1944 and its combat debut with 617 Squadron was on the night of June 8/9, 1944 against a key railroad tunnel in the Loire valley. The Tallboy bombs were not used against the Heavy Crossbow sites until after the start of Operation *Eisbär* and are described in more detail below.

Operation *Eisbär* delayed

Regardless of the delays imposed on the missile campaign by the Crossbow bombing, the start of Operation *Eisbär* was continually postponed by a lack of missiles and support equipment. Manufacture of the FZG.76 was scheduled to begin at the Volkswagen plant at Fallersleben and at Fieseler in Kassel-Bettenhausen in August 1943. Some of the delay

A formation of B-24 Liberators of the 2nd Bombardment Division on a mission to France in late 1943. The aircraft in the foreground, B-24H "Our Baby" of the 579th BS, 392nd Bomb Group was lost during the mission against the Watten Heavy Crossbow site on February 2, 1944.

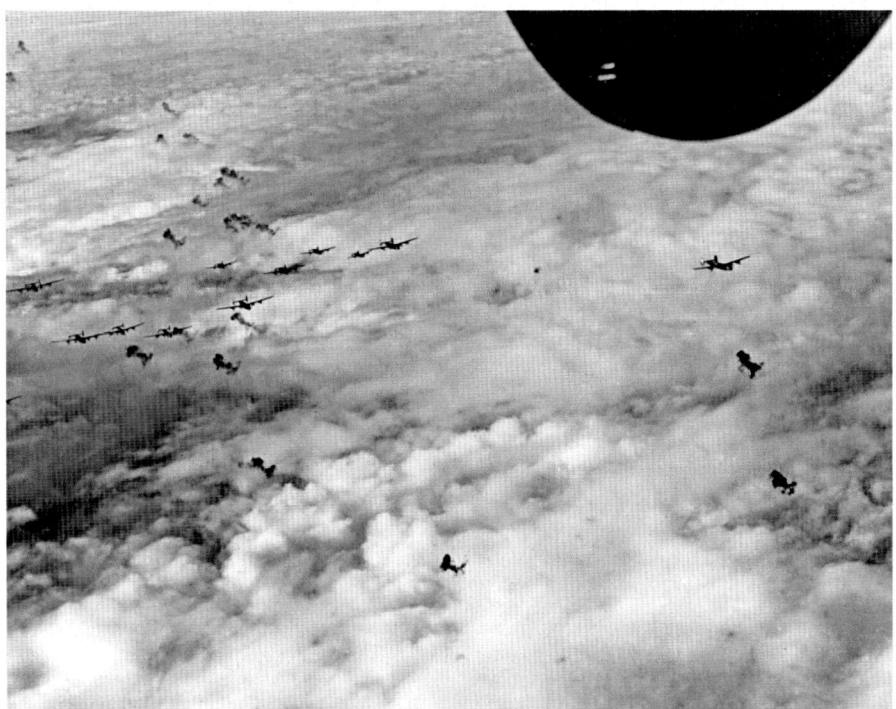

Flak bursts among a formation of B-24 Liberators of the 2nd Bombardment Division during Mission 220 over the Heavy Crossbow site at Siracourt on February 12, 1944. This mission involved 97 B-24 bombers from the 93rd, 389th, and 392nd Bomb Groups, delivering 279 tons of bombs. A total of 29 aircraft suffered flak damage during the attack.

was caused by the priorities of the German aircraft industry. Armaments minister Albert Speer continued to favor the army's A-4 missile. The Luftwaffe decision to emphasize fighter construction undermined the FZG.76 program since it was considered a bomber substitute. These initial delays were not entirely detrimental as the FZG.76 was still not technologically mature. Through August 1943, only 60 percent of the test launches were successful and, in particular, the Askania guidance system was still not dependable. In December 1943, guidance problems and other issues were still so severe that if the FZG.76 had been launched against London that month as planned, fewer than one in six would have reached their destination solely due to technical flaws.

Further adding to the delay was the RAF bombing campaign against the Ruhr industrial region. An October 22, 1943 RAF raid on the Fieseler plant near Kassel shut down its FZG.76 assembly line, leaving only the Volkswagen plant in Fallersleben. Production was further delayed by the endless stream of changes and modifications to the design. The first batch of production missiles used riveted construction for the wings which tended to rip off on launch. The new lightweight stamped steel wing-rib, introduced to cure the problem, proved too weak and the first batch of 1,400 missile sets had to be scrapped. At the end of November 1943, production was halted until the problems could be remedied and significant production did not resume until March 1944, after the production faults had been ironed out.

To test the new series-production missiles, as well as to gauge the level of troop training, a series of test launches were conducted at Zempin on May 10–13, 1944 using crews from FR.155W. Of the 29 FZG.76 s launched, 22 performed satisfactorily, two missiles flew too far, two crashed prematurely, and three were lost to tracking radar for an overall 76 percent success rate.

During the period from initial deployment of FR.155W in France until the start of Operation *Eisbär*, considerable attention was paid to lingering tactical issues, especially the lack of any means to determine whether the missiles were striking their targets. Various technical means such as acoustic listening posts were tried but were not particularly reliable.

At the beginning of 1944, the FZG.76 was not mature enough for combat use because of a variety of technical and manufacturing flaws. Even when Operation *Eisbär* started in June 1944, about a third of the missiles crashed prematurely due to an array of technical problems.

In the end, the small FuG 23 radio transmitter was fitted to a proportion of missiles, and the signals triangulated from posts along the French coast to determine the missiles' terminal location. Test results were far from ideal but the device was better than nothing. There were also schemes to infiltrate agents into London to observe the fall of missiles, but this was largely snuffed out by efficient British counter-intelligence measures.

In spite of the problems affecting the FZG.76, the technical difficulties with the A-4 ballistic missile and HDP gun were even more acute. The seed of the eventual A-4 missile regiment, Lehr und Versuchsbatterie 444 (Training and Experimental Battery 444) was created in July 1943 and deployed to the Waffen-SS Heidelager training ground, a former Polish artillery range near Bliżna in Poland. Batterie 444 began field launches of pre-production A-4A missiles starting on November 5, 1943. The training launches were a fiasco. On several occasions, the missile engine failed shortly after launch, and the missile toppled over and destroyed the launch pad. Others lifted off properly but then exploded overhead. The most alarming results were the missiles that had flown the full range; most broke up in flight during the final descent. Up to the end of March 1944 when the A-4 was supposed to be ready for combat, there had been 57 launches at Blizna, of which only 26 actually got into the air. Of these, only seven reached the ground and only four in the target area. Not a single missile with a functional warhead had impacted; all had disintegrated in the air. The missile fuselage had to be completely redesigned and the definitive series-production version of the A-4C was not ready for trial launches until August 30, 1944.

The HDP gun presented a more modest technical challenge, but the projectile design was so inept that it spun uncontrollably after firing. The initial production run of projectiles had to be scrapped and a new configuration designed from scratch. As a result, there was no satisfactory ammunition for the HDP gun available in the summer of 1944 when Operation *Eisbär* was supposed to start. In the event, the guns were never installed at the Mimoyecques site.

Operation *Eisbär* begins

Wachtel's headquarters was notified of the Allied amphibious landings in Normandy on the morning of June 6, 1944 and the various guard units assigned to the regiment were activated. Guards still located at the old Stellung-System.I were transferred to the operational Stellung-System.II due to concerns that Allied paratrooper attacks could begin at any moment. Wachtel's headquarters moved from Merlemont to the main combat command

In late May 1944, FR.155W began to deploy the launch rails and other structures to their modified sites. This is Site 152 of II./FR.155W located near Vignacourt to the northeast of Amiens, and identified by Allied intelligence as Noball XI/A/154. The modified sites required few new structures besides the launch rail itself (P) and the magnetic orientation hut (Q) identified on this overhead reconnaissance photo. This site was hit on July 2, 1944 by the 486th Bomb Group and destroyed.

An FZG.76 on its Walter 2.3 launch rail. The device near the fuselage side is the Anlassgerät which transmitted electrical commands to the missile from the control bunker. Behind the launch rail is the Dampferzeuger gas generator dolly.

center at Saleux near Amiens. At 1745 hours, Heinemann's 65.Korps issued the command "Rumpelkammer" (Junk Room). This code word meant that Operation *Eisbär* would begin in ten days. The two main field ammunition depots, Nordpol and Leopold, began transporting the launch ramps to Stellung-System.II. By this stage, all but eight of the new sites had been completed as far as the basic construction was concerned and FR.155W had 873 missiles on hand in the battalion depots.

Although preparations for Operation *Overlord* had ended Allied air attacks on the launch sites, Allied air strikes against the French railway system caused some significant losses to FR.155W. Allied fighter bombers operating against the Rochy-Condé railway station and the rail lines near Beauvais struck a train carrying 270,000 liters of aviation fuel intended for the regiment, along with another rail transport carrying FZG.76 missiles.

On June 11, the principal officers in charge of Operation *Eisbär* met at Heinemann's 65.Korps headquarters and were instructed to begin the FZG.76 launches on the night of June 12/13. Heinemann had decided to start the attacks earlier than the 10-day preparation period owing to pressure from Berlin. He seriously underestimated the chaotic conditions on the highways and railroad lines in France caused by Allied air attacks on all major transportation networks. Wachtel objected to the premature start date and indicated that the regiment would not be ready until June 20. Heinemann insisted that the initial launches take place.

The launches on June 12/13 were a chaotic mess. A rail-yard near the Saleux command post was heavily bombed that night, which knocked out all the land-lines to the launch sites. This delayed the first launches to 2300 hours. The launch batteries reported that 63 of the 72 launch sites were ready to fire. Of the first salvo, only nine missiles actually left the launchers, and not one of these reached England; many crashed a short distance from the launchers. The second salvo, scheduled for 0330 hours was only slightly more successful. Ten missiles were launched, of which four immediately crashed in the vicinity of the launchers. Two more crashed into the Channel, and four reached England. One landed in London near

Bethnal Green at 0418 hours. Churchill's science adviser and long-time *Crossbow* skeptic, Lord Cherwell, remarked that "The mountain hath groaned and given forth a mouse!"

Heinemann ordered a cessation of launches and immediate camouflage of all launch sites until an inquiry could be conducted. It became quite clear that the launch troops, although very enthusiastic, had taken too many shortcuts to get the launch sites ready for the attack. Some of the sites had lacked any form of lighting and so were unable to conduct nighttime loading and launching procedures. In addition, IV./FR.155W did not have any of the sodium permanganate needed to operate the gas generator for the launcher.

After a few days of preparation, the next attack on the night of June 15/16 was far more successful. The first launch began at 2316 hours on June 15. There were several mishaps during the launching with explosions at six of the ramps, often from the volatile fuel used in the gas generator trailer. A total of 55 launchers fired 294 missiles, of which 45 crashed after launch, 144 reached the English coast, and 73 fell on London. Seven were shot down by RAF fighters and 25 by antiaircraft guns. Radar tracking of the missiles indicated that they had been accurately targeted and a Luftwaffe reconnaissance aircraft dispatched towards London reported that he had observed a fire glow over London far greater than any previous IX.Fliegerkorps attack.

Attacks continued over the next several nights since it was felt that missiles would be less subject to fighter interception. On its own initiative, 65.Korps also launched 53 missiles against the ports in the Portsmouth–Southampton area on June 26, hoping to disrupt Allied invasion shipping. When higher headquarters was informed of the port attacks, Heinemann was reprimanded for violating Hitler's orders to concentrate on London.

The summer crisis

The small-scale attacks on the night of June 12/13 led to a War Cabinet meeting in London to discuss options. The source of the missiles was still uncertain. Allied intelligence believed that most of the ski sites were no longer functional, and there was some suspicion that the missiles came either from the "modified" sites or from the Heavy Crossbow sites. Recent aerial photography over the Pas-de-Calais revealed a sudden blossoming of the "modified" sites as the launchers were finally deployed.

On the afternoon of Saturday June 17, 1944, a V-1 buzz bomb landed on a street in St. John's Hill, Battersea, London damaging the Surrey Hounds public house, two passing trolley buses, and numerous homes and businesses; one person was killed and many more were wounded.

There was growing resistance from the air commanders to divert missions to attack the ski sites. Instead, Spaatz wanted to shift the focus to an attack on the missile supply network and the German industry manufacturing the missiles. The problem with the latter mission was that Allied intelligence had very little precise information on the location of the missile plants or their sub-contractors. There was a belief that hydrogen peroxide plants were a key industry since the earlier Hs.293 antiship missile had used this for its rocket engine. In fact, the FZG.76 did not use this oxidizer for fuel, but did use it in the steam catapult of the launch system.

Eighth Air Force had successfully crushed the Luftwaffe fighter force with Operation *Pointblank* in the late winter and early spring of 1944, but had been diverted in May and June 1944 to support Operation *Overlord*. Spaatz and Doolittle were wary of futile attacks on the devastated ski sites, and wanted to return the focus to Germany, both to keep the Luftwaffe suppressed as well as to continue new missions against the German fuel industry and the industrial transportation network. Both the 2nd Tactical Air Force and Ninth Air Force were now under Leigh-Mallory's AEAF command, and they were intensely focused on providing air support for the Allied ground forces in Normandy. RAF Bomber Command remained inactive in the *Crossbow* battles, though 617 Squadron was preparing to use the new Tallboy bombs to strike the Heavy Crossbow sites.

The much more successful missile attacks on the night of June 15/16 completely changed the situation. Churchill held a meeting of the War Cabinet on the morning of June 16. The previous Crossbow Committee of the JIC had been deactivated earlier in the year and its functions largely turned over to the British Air Ministry. Churchill ordered the creation of a new Crossbow Committee under the War Cabinet, and he personally led it during the first weeks of the new crisis. On June 18, Churchill visited the SHAEF headquarters at Teddington, and stressed to Eisenhower and his deputy commander, Air Marshal Arthur Tedder, the need to elevate Operation *Crossbow* to the first priority in the Allied air campaign.

Diver Down! A V-1 descends into central London with the spire of St. Martin's in the Field visible on the far left and the Methodist Central Hall in Westminster in the foreground.

Air Defence Great Britain

On the morning of June 16, the War Cabinet activated the "Diver" air defense plan. Antiaircraft Artillery Command developed the Diver plan in December 1943 but, when the flying bombs failed to appear, the gun belt shriveled due to the demand for more antiaircraft guns for Normandy. Instead, fighter aircraft were given a more prominent role in the scheme. To thicken the gun belt to respond to the new threat, more AA guns were transferred from elsewhere in Britain. By June 28 there were 376 heavy guns and 576 light guns of the British Army in the Diver belt protecting London, plus a further 560 light guns of the RAF Regiment and two US Army radar-directed AA battalions. A balloon barrage was added on June 22, increasing from 480 balloons eventually to 1,400 balloons. Due to the low-altitude approach of the Doodlebugs, it was hoped that the steel cables below the balloons would cause any missiles that struck them to lose their wings and crash before reaching London.

By mid-July 1944, FR.155W had fired about 4,000 missiles. Only about 3,000 actually reached the air defense corridor to London and 1,240 were knocked down, 924 by fighters, 261 by guns, and 55 by balloons. Even though a third of the missiles were being shot down by the London defenses in early July, this was still not good enough. A significant problem for the air defense was the proper mixture of guns and aircraft. When fighters were present, the guns had to remain silent. To improve the air defense, the antiaircraft and fighter commands agreed to reorganize and introduce improved equipment. The antiaircraft guns were moved to the coast where the new American SCR-584 gun-laying radars would have an unobstructed view of the missiles as they approached, permitting earlier and more accurate target tracking. The move took place on July 16–17, 1944 and required re-laying almost two thousand miles of telephone cable and moving thousands of tons of weapons, ammunition, and equipment. This created a free-fire zone for the guns and a safe corridor for the fighters to operate.

On July 16–17, 1944, London's antiaircraft gun belt moved to the coast to prevent fratricide with British fighters and to improve gun and radar tracking of the approaching V-1 buzz bombs. Here, a 40mm Bofors battery is alerted on the approach of "Doodlebugs" in August 1944.

Barrage balloons proved to be a simple but effective countermeasure to the low-flying V-1, accounting for 231 buzz bombs, or about 6 percent of the missiles brought down by all defenses. A portion of the late-production V-1 missiles had a special reinforced wing intended to cut the balloon cables. Here, civil defense workers examine the wreckage of a crashed V-1, with a crumpled wing evident in the left foreground.

The US Army also added a further improvement with the first combat use of its top-secret "variable-time" (VT) fuze, which proved to be more than five times as effective as conventional fuzes. The VT fuze was a miniaturized radar proximity fuze that detonated the projectile when it approached closest to the target. The US Army had been reluctant to use the new design, fearing that if any fell into enemy hands, a German copy could wreak havoc among the Allied heavy bombers over the Reich. The improvement was dramatic. During the third week of July, the guns accounted for half of all flying bombs reaching the London area and continued to improve, reaching 83 percent by the end of August.

The redesigned air defense zone proved much more effective, downing about 40 percent of the Doodlebugs before the move, and nearly 60 percent after the move. The peak V-1 assault occurred on August 3 when 316 missiles were launched, of which about 220 reached London. The number launched against London subsequently began to fall due to the growing problems of supplying the sites, and the gradual loss of the launching areas as the Allied armies advanced in Normandy.

Operation *Crossbow* Phase II

Regardless of Harris's previous resistance to participation in *Crossbow*, Churchill made it clear that RAF Bomber Command would now have to take a role since the two tactical air forces were too tightly engaged in the campaign in Normandy. Harris remained skeptical of the value of attacking the launch sites, so the initial missions on the night of June 16/17 concentrated on the Heavy Crossbow and supply sites with 315 sorties dropping 1,423 tons of bombs. In June 1944, RAF Bomber Command took over the brunt of Phase II of the *Crossbow* campaign, dropping 15,907 tons of bombs in 4,057 sorties. Bomber Command's *Crossbow* missions took up nearly 30 percent of its total combat activity in the second half of June 1944.

The Eighth Air Force at first hesitated to begin missions because of the overcast weather conditions. Under intense pressure from both Churchill and Eisenhower, Doolittle ordered the start of attacks on June 16 with 183 B-24s from the 2nd Bombardment Division dropping 477 tons of bombs. Since the targets were completely obscured by cloud cover, non-visual aiming techniques were used such as the Gee-H radio navigation system. The missions continued on June 19, and included attacks on electrical power stations near the Crossbow sites for the first time in the hopes of indirectly halting their operations. The Eighth Air Force *Crossbow* missions in the last two weeks of June totaled 2,149 sorties and 5,524 tons of bombs.

A spectacular firework display as a night-time V-1 attack is greeted by British antiaircraft fire near the Channel coast. Although FR.155W favored night attacks during the early phase of Operation *Eisbär*, opinions changed in late summer due to the belief that night launches made it easier for British fighters to locate and intercept the buzz bombs.

LEFT The priority of *Crossbow* over other strategic bomber missions prompted an acrimonious debate among senior Allied air commanders in the summer of 1944, especially the deputy SHAEF commander, Air Chief Marshal Tedder seen here on the left and USSTAF commander Lt. Gen. Carl Spaatz seen here on the right. The officer behind them is Maj. Gen. Ralph Royce, deputy commander of the Ninth Air Force.

Chaplain (Capt.) Michael Ragan conducts a religious ceremony for the crews of the 322nd BS, 91st Bomb Group at Bassingbourn in June 1944. This B-17G, named "Fifinella," had flown 30 missions up to this point and was lost to flak on its 54th mission on August 13, 1944 while bombing a bridge in France.

Although the British Air Ministry continued to frown on low-altitude attacks, VIII Fighter Command began to experiment with low-altitude attacks by fighters dropping auxiliary fuel tanks with a 2lb incendiary bomb attached to ignite the gasoline. The first such attack was conducted by a P-38 of the 55th Fighter Group on the Fôret de Boulogne on July 14. The attacks had mixed results, and VIII Fighter Command dropped the improvised firebomb attacks in favor of low-altitude attacks using bombs and machine-gun fire. The Eighth Air Force had a substantial escort fighter force, and on days when they were not needed on missions into Germany, they were directed to operations over the Pas-de-Calais to support Operation *Crossbow*. The fighters were assigned to conduct patrols along railway lines in the hopes of interdicting the transfer of missiles. Ninth Air Force was also diverted to *Crossbow* again, and its medium bombers conducted about 1,500 sorties with 2,000 tons of bombs.

The targeting lists provided by the Air Ministry fluctuated due to a lack of good intelligence on the actual source of the missile attacks. The target priority lists continued to fluctuate including the battered Heavy Crossbow bunkers, old ski sites, and sites thought to be part of the new modified launch site system.

The bombing in the last two weeks of June 1944 had no apparent effect on the German missile launches, and indeed, the FZG.76 attacks appeared to be intensifying. This led to vigorous protests from both heavy bomber commanders, Harris and Doolittle, who became increasingly concerned that vital bomber resources were being wasted simply to satisfy the political demands for more and more *Crossbow* missions, regardless of their effectiveness. Harris demanded photographic evidence before scheduling attacks on the modified sites. Brigadier General Frederic Smith, deputy senior air staff of the AEAF, informed the Air Ministry that he intended to employ the bomber force against oil targets and bridges in France rather than continue *Crossbow* missions that were "unjustified by prior photographic reconnaissance." Coningham attempted to withdraw the 2nd TAF entirely from the *Crossbow* mission, due to the heavy commitment of his aircraft in support of the Normandy campaign.

Many of the Eighth Air Force's *Crossbow* missions in late June had been conducted using unobserved blind-bombing techniques which were inherently inaccurate against precision targets. As a result, Eighth Air Force recommended that their *Crossbow* missions be suspended until weather permitted visual bombing and that, instead of small-scale attacks in poor weather, a mass attack should be conducted once the weather cleared. There were also suggestions that the Eighth Air Force and Bomber Command conduct a series of retaliatory raids on Berlin, an option first supported, but eventually rejected by Eisenhower's second in command, Air Chief Marshal Tedder. Spaatz suggested that the electrical network in the Pas-de-Calais be attacked since he argued that a loss of electrical power to the Heavy Crossbow sites and major supply sites would render them non-functional. As mentioned earlier, these attacks began in late June 1944. Spaatz also initiated a special attack unit dubbed Aphrodite, detailed below, to attack the Heavy Crossbow sites.

RAF armorers move a recalcitrant bomb trolley through the mud to arm their Mitchell bombers at a forward field on the Continent. The 2nd Tactical Air Force played a smaller role in Phase II of Operation *Crossbow* due to their heavy role in supporting the Allied armies.

ABOVE A Mitchell of 180 Squadron, 2nd Tactical Air Force, takes off from RAF Dunsfold on a mission in August 1944. (Library and Archives Canada, MIKAN 4447477)

RIGHT "Fanny Ferkin II" a Lancaster BII of 514 Squadron, lands at Deenethorpe in May 1944 on a familiarization tour with the 401st Bomb Group. The 514 Squadron was heavily involved in Phase II of Operation *Crossbow* in June and July 1944.

The crisis intensified in early July when FR.155W managed to launch a thousand FZG.76 missiles during the week of July 2–8, of which 820 reached Britain. The growing intensity of the German missile attacks and the apparent failure of Operation *Crossbow* to stifle the attacks prompted the War Cabinet to consider other options. Chief among these was a series of retaliatory bomber raids against German cities. Consideration was also given to more extreme measures, including the use of gas weapons against the missile sites. Eisenhower opposed the use of gas warfare, fully appreciating that, once initiated, it would probably spread to being used by both sides with horrific consequences. He also opposed announcing any specific retaliatory missions against German cities since it would serve only to affirm the effectiveness of the new German weapons.

On July 6, Maj. Gen. Frederick Anderson, the USSTAF's deputy operations commander, forwarded the War Cabinet a comprehensive paper recommending a reconsideration of Operation *Crossbow* that suggested a balanced program of countermeasures including an emphasis on Crossbow supply sites, instead of the elusive launch sites; attacks on the German missile industry; and an intensification of antiaircraft guns and fighter defense against the missiles being undertaken by ADGB (Air Defence Great Britain). Due to frustration over the poor targeting assignments coming from the Air Ministry, on July 8, Anderson proposed the creation of a Joint *Crossbow* Committee to end the Air Ministry monopoly of targeting assignments, as well as a shift in decision-making away from the bureaucrats in London to the British and American field commands. This recommendation was supported by Spaatz and other senior US commanders and efforts were made to win Eisenhower's and Tedder's support. This resulted in the creation of the Joint *Crossbow* Target Priorities Committee on July 21. This committee had only advisory powers, and was often overruled by Tedder due to intense political pressure from the British Air Ministry and the War Cabinet.

The Phase II attacks gradually shifted the emphasis to the supply sites. From June 12 to August 1, the supply sites absorbed 72 percent of the bomb tonnage, 555 sorties and 2,019 tons of bombs, while 13 launch sites were attacked totaling 231 sorties with 779 tons or 28 percent of the total. The early target sets placed considerable emphasis on the Fôret-de-Nieppe, a large forest near the launch sites that was used as a forward depot for future A-4 ballistic missile operations. This area was repeatedly hit by RAF Bomber Command starting in late July, eventually totaling 3,400 tons. The Nordpol depot near Neucourt was first hit on June 22 by the 447th Bomb Group, 3rd Bombardment Division of the Eighth Air Force with 70 B-17s dropping 207.5 tons of bombs. British and American attacks against this site continued through August, leaving a lunar landscape. The site was finally

A Handley Page Halifax Mk. III, of 425 "Alouette" Squadron, No. 6 Group, on the taxiway at RAF Tholthorpe. This French-Canadian squadron flew on several *Crossbow* missions in the summer of 1944. This particular aircraft, coded KW-T, completed 60 missions through February 8, 1945. (Library and Archives Canada, MIKAN 4752281)

abandoned on August 21–22. The Leopold depot near Saint-Leu-d'Esserent was hit by RAF Bomber Command on the night of July 4, causing substantial damage and the site was hit repeatedly to prevent repair. A follow-on attack on July 7 brought the total to 3,000 tons of bombs, collapsing many sections of the tunnel and devastating the road network leading to the depot. The Richard tunnel depot at Rilly-la-Montagne was hit by Bomber Command on July 17 and July 31, largely sealing the tunnel. The use of Tallboy attacks against these sites is detailed below. These attacks forced the Luftwaffe to disperse the depots into a larger number of smaller facilities.

Although the launch sites received less priority than during *Crossbow* Phase I, there were still a significant number of bombing attacks. Eventually, about 20,000 tons of bombs were dropped on the modified sites, with the heavy bombers accounting for most, as detailed in the table.

ATTACKS ON THE MODIFIED SITES BY COMMAND		
Command	Tons	Sites with Category A Damage
Bomber Command	14,000	12
Eighth Air Force	5,000	11
Tactical Air Forces	1,200	6

The first meeting of the Joint *Crossbow* Committee recommended that attacks on modified sites be limited to harassing attacks, all attacks on old ski sites be halted, all attacks on the Heavy Crossbow sites be ended except for *Aphrodite* missions, and that priority be given to the attack of three missile storage depots and seven missile-associated plants in Germany. Tedder did not agree with the recommendation to end heavy bomber missions against the launch sites, and he continued to pressure the bomber commands to attack the modified sites.

In frustration over the issue, Doolittle occasionally chose to ignore Tedder's requests for Eighth Air Force attacks on the launch sites. The implicit policy by Spaatz and Doolittle was to conduct *Crossbow* missions only on days when weather prevented missions against priority targets in Germany. The matter came to a head on August 15 after Doolittle assigned Eighth Air Force to strike targets in the Leipzig area. When asked why no *Crossbow* missions were scheduled that day, Doolittle told Tedder that there were no Crossbow sites near Leipzig. Dissension over Tedder's repeated instructions for attacks on the launch sites had much the same results on August 17 when Doolittle decided to strike key rail bridges in France instead, hoping to isolate the launch sites from the Luftwaffe missile depots in neighboring western Germany.

Several Handley Page Halifax Mk. IIIs of the RCAF's 425 Squadron, No. 6 Group, begin to taxi forward at Tholthorpe during a mission in 1944. The group flew 25,353 operational sorties and dropped 86,503 tons of bombs in 1944, including the summer 1944 *Crossbow* campaign. (Library and Archives Canada, MIKAN 4752276)

The Eighth Air Force generally shifted its targeting in July and August away from the small and difficult modified sites and towards fuel and missile storage facilities. When it was discovered that missile fuel was being stockpiled at Luftwaffe airbases, these sites were hit as well. The shift in targeting is evident in the war diary of FR.155W which estimated that its launch sites had been subjected to about 235 sorties daily in late June, 220 daily in early July, and 90 daily in late July 1944. During *Crossbow* Phase II from June 16 to the end of August 1944, the Eighth Air Force conducted 4,105 sorties against Noball sites and dropped 10,677 tons of bombs.

Tallboy attacks on the Heavy Crossbow sites

The mysterious Heavy Crossbow sites remained a major source of anxiety for Churchill and the War Cabinet. Since the ski sites had been largely destroyed by Phase I of the *Crossbow* attacks, the sudden appearance of buzz bombs in June 1944 was initially attributed to these sites. Even when it became apparent that the attacks were being launched from the modified sites, there was still a concern that the "concrete monsters" would be home to the terrifying new A-4 ballistic missile. As a result, both RAF Bomber Command and the Eighth Air Force continued to bomb these sites. Unknown to *Crossbow* planners, Hitler had ordered an end to the construction of these sites at the beginning of July 1944. For deception purposes, some external construction work continued in hopes of wasting Allied bombs.

There was some recognition that bombing to date had not penetrated any of the hardened roofs of the main structures, so the Heavy Crossbow sites were among the first targets of 617 Squadron dropping the new Tallboy penetrating bombs. The first of these was a daylight attack on Watten on June 19, 1944, by 18 Lancasters of 617 Squadron supported by two Mosquitoes as marker aircraft along with an escort of 47 Spitfire IX fighters. For a variety of reasons, no hits were scored on the main structure. The 617 Squadron returned on July 25, scoring two direct hits on the roof that caused minor internal damage. One problem with the Tallboy bomb was that it could reliably penetrate the thick concrete roofs, but in the process the fuze was sometimes damaged and so the high explosives did not detonate after penetration was made. This substantially reduced the amount of damage that might have occurred. Watten had been so badly cratered by the numerous *Crossbow* attacks that it became almost impossible to continue construction work at the site, and work was finally abandoned after this raid.

The next target on the list was the neighboring A-4 missile site at Wizernes. A mission on June 20 was aborted due to adverse weather conditions and rescheduled for June 24 using 16 Lancasters plus escorts and marking aircraft. Once again, there were several hits near the large dome covering the missile preparation cavern, but no direct impacts. The 617 Squadron returned on July 17 with 16 Lancasters. There were no direct hits on the dome, but several hits near the edge completely undermined the structure and forced the abandonment of any further construction of the missile gallery.

The third target was the FZG.76 site at Siracourt. This facility was being constructed using earth fill under the roof, and this had not yet been excavated. The first attack on June 25 by 17 Lancasters was successful with one bomb penetrating the roof but not detonating inside, and a near miss that damaged a burster slab on the side. Another mission was launched on August 1, but it was aborted due to weather conditions. Like Watten, this site had been so heavily bombed that any further construction work proved to be impossible.

The HDP gun site at Mimoyecques was targeted on July 6 by 17 Lancasters with supporting marker Mosquitoes and fighter escorts. This was another successful mission

Tallboy attack on Wizernes Heavy Crossbow site, June 24, 1944

The usual tactic for 617 Squadron when employing the Tallboy bomb was to approach the target in a gaggle with the aircraft traveling in pairs with the leader ahead and the trailing aircraft behind and to the right. Each pair was separated from one another vertically by a distance of about a hundred feet with the higher pairs behind the pair below. During the attack run, the formation was flying at an altitude of 16,000 to 17,200 feet. The gaggle was designed to place the formation over the target in a compact group, while at the same time avoiding the risk of collision or of a bomb from one of the upper aircraft striking an aircraft below. The bomb release on this mission started at 1750 hours with a near-simultaneous release by the first five aircraft. The next ten aircraft released their Tallboy bombs at 1757 to 1803 hours. This attack undermined the dome over the Wizernes missile assembly hall, leading to the abandonment of any further work at the site.

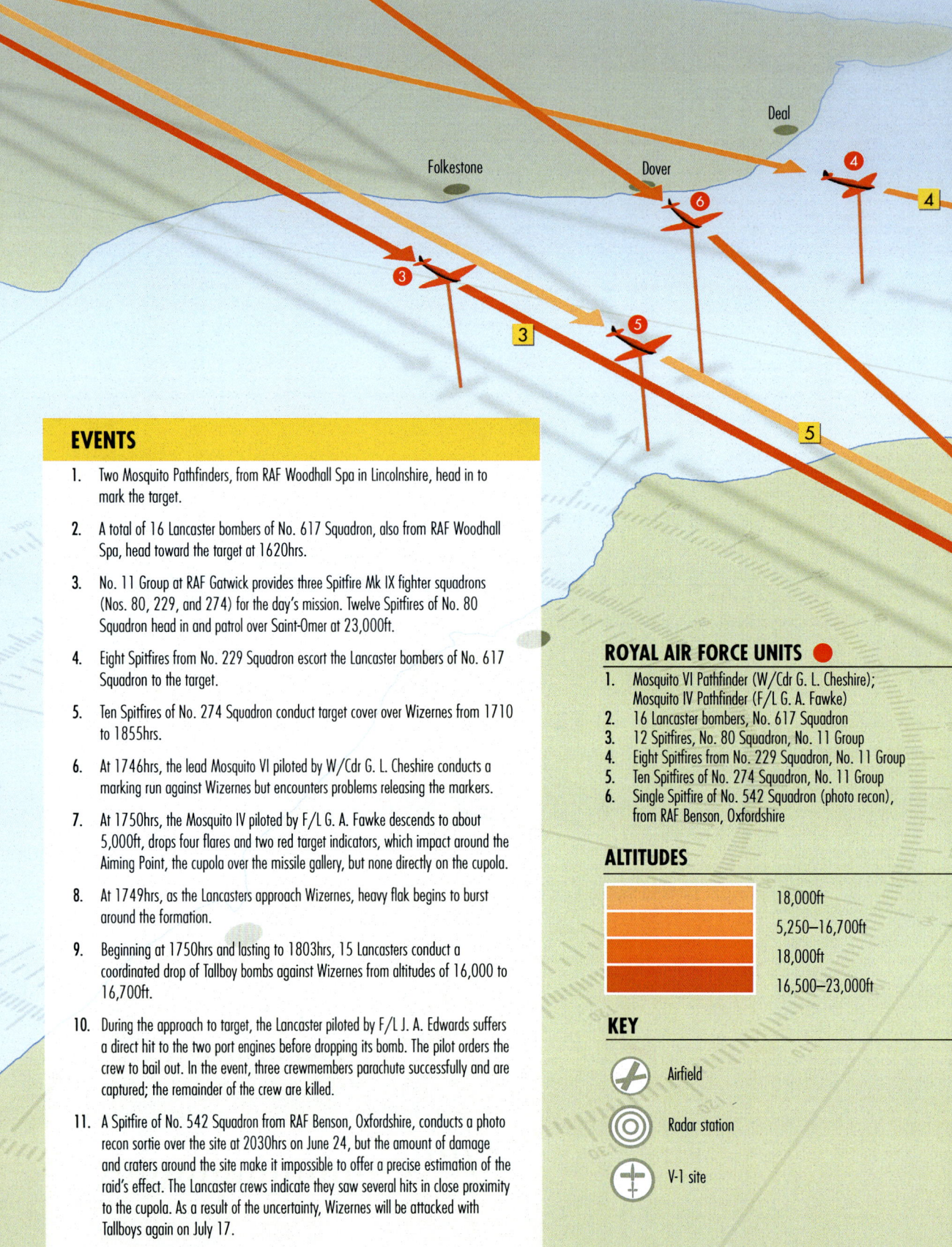

EVENTS

1. Two Mosquito Pathfinders, from RAF Woodhall Spa in Lincolnshire, head in to mark the target.

2. A total of 16 Lancaster bombers of No. 617 Squadron, also from RAF Woodhall Spa, head toward the target at 1620hrs.

3. No. 11 Group at RAF Gatwick provides three Spitfire Mk IX fighter squadrons (Nos. 80, 229, and 274) for the day's mission. Twelve Spitfires of No. 80 Squadron head in and patrol over Saint-Omer at 23,000ft.

4. Eight Spitfires from No. 229 Squadron escort the Lancaster bombers of No. 617 Squadron to the target.

5. Ten Spitfires of No. 274 Squadron conduct target cover over Wizernes from 1710 to 1855hrs.

6. At 1746hrs, the lead Mosquito VI piloted by W/Cdr G. L. Cheshire conducts a marking run against Wizernes but encounters problems releasing the markers.

7. At 1750hrs, the Mosquito IV piloted by F/L G. A. Fawke descends to about 5,000ft, drops four flares and two red target indicators, which impact around the Aiming Point, the cupola over the missile gallery, but none directly on the cupola.

8. At 1749hrs, as the Lancasters approach Wizernes, heavy flak begins to burst around the formation.

9. Beginning at 1750hrs and lasting to 1803hrs, 15 Lancasters conduct a coordinated drop of Tallboy bombs against Wizernes from altitudes of 16,000 to 16,700ft.

10. During the approach to target, the Lancaster piloted by F/L J. A. Edwards suffers a direct hit to the two port engines before dropping its bomb. The pilot orders the crew to bail out. In the event, three crewmembers parachute successfully and are captured; the remainder of the crew are killed.

11. A Spitfire of No. 542 Squadron from RAF Benson, Oxfordshire, conducts a photo recon sortie over the site at 2030hrs on June 24, but the amount of damage and craters around the site make it impossible to offer a precise estimation of the raid's effect. The Lancaster crews indicate they saw several hits in close proximity to the cupola. As a result of the uncertainty, Wizernes will be attacked with Tallboys again on July 17.

ROYAL AIR FORCE UNITS

1. Mosquito VI Pathfinder (W/Cdr G. L. Cheshire); Mosquito IV Pathfinder (F/L G. A. Fawke)
2. 16 Lancaster bombers, No. 617 Squadron
3. 12 Spitfires, No. 80 Squadron, No. 11 Group
4. Eight Spitfires from No. 229 Squadron, No. 11 Group
5. Ten Spitfires of No. 274 Squadron, No. 11 Group
6. Single Spitfire of No. 542 Squadron (photo recon), from RAF Benson, Oxfordshire

ALTITUDES

- 18,000ft
- 5,250–16,700ft
- 18,000ft
- 16,500–23,000ft

KEY

- Airfield
- Radar station
- V-1 site

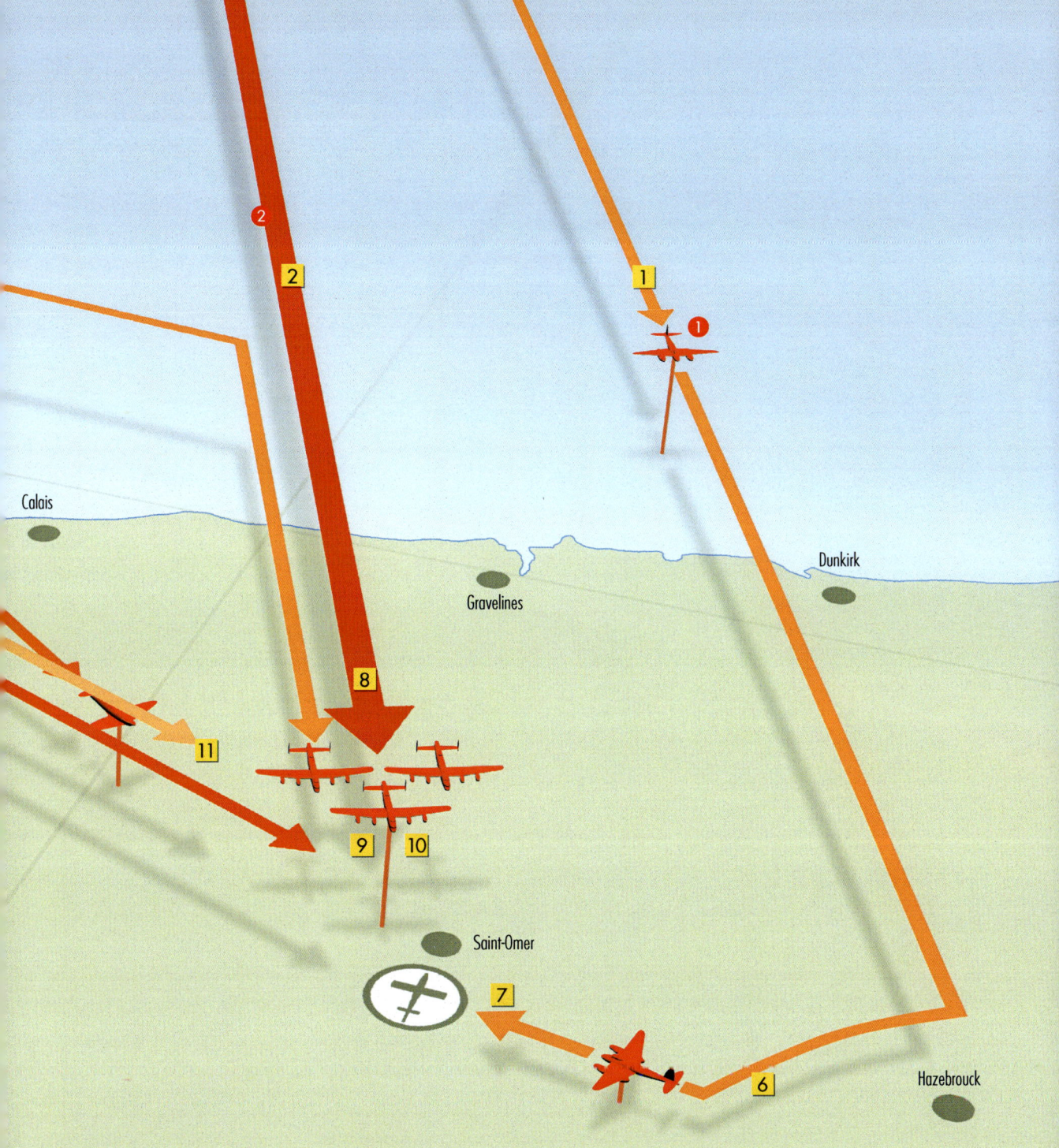

Tallboy attack on Wizernes Heavy Crossbow site
June 24, 1944

A pair of Tallboy bombs are prepared by RAF armorers at a bomb dump. These 12,000lb bombs had a front casing made of high-strength steel to withstand impact with reinforced concrete. The Tallboy was designed to be dropped from an optimal altitude of 18,000ft (5,500m) in order to impact the target at a speed of 750mph (1,210km/h) to maximize penetration.

A view of the Kraftwerk Nordwest bunker near Watten, shortly after its capture by Canadian troops in September 1944. This was one of the most heavily bombed Crossbow sites, as is evident from the numerous craters around the facility. (Library and Archives Canada, PA-174460)

with one of the Tallboys striking the concrete slab over the gun battery, penetrating inside and detonating. About 2,000 construction workers and engineers were killed during the attack. Most of the casualties occurred when the blast ruptured a neighboring underground water table, flooding the air raid shelters in the lower galleries.

Besides the attacks on the Heavy Crossbow sites, 617 Squadron was also sent to attack several of the FZG.76 missile storage sites since they were located in caves and tunnels that were impervious to smaller bombs. In many cases, these were combined raids with the sites being hit first by Lancasters dropping conventional bombs, followed by a 617 Squadron strike using Tallboys. On July 4, 17 Lancasters attacked the Leopold depot at Saint-Leu-d'Esserent, located in prewar mushroom caves. The attack was very successful, with one Tallboy hitting the cave entrance, collapsing it. There were an estimated 800 German personnel entombed in the attack, some of the heaviest casualties of Operation *Crossbow* aside from the Mimoyecques attack.

The next storage site attacked with Tallboys was the Richard depot at Rilly-la-Montagne on July 31, another combined attack beginning with Lancaster squadrons' conventional bombs followed by 16 Lancasters with Tallboys. One of the tunnel entrances was completely blocked while the other end was so heavily cratered that access was impossible.

The enormous power of the Tallboy bomb is evident in this aerial photograph of the Kraftwerk Nordwest bunker near Watten. One of the impact craters can be seen in the left foreground.

Operation *Aphrodite*

The other special weapon used against the Heavy Crossbow sites was a new type of guided missile based on war-weary bombers. In May 1944, Doolittle had come up with the idea of packing "Weary Willie" B-17 and B-24 bombers with high explosive, and then flying them by remote control into targets in France or Germany. This task was handed off to the Air Materiel Command at Wright Field, Ohio where it was called Project Castor.

When the first wave of FZG.76 s struck London in early June 1944, the matter of destroying the Heavy Crossbow sites took on greater urgency. On June 20, USSTAF contacted Wright Field and requested that the equipment associated with Project Castor be rushed to Britain as soon as possible. In the meantime, engineering officers of USSTAF concluded that it would be possible to modify war-weary B-17 bombers locally using the radio-control system associated with the AZON (Azimuth Only) guided bomb that was being used on an experimental basis by the Eighth Air Force. Since the AZON equipment operated in only one axis, two control systems were used to provide both azimuth and elevation control. As a result, the modified controls were dubbed "Double AZON." The codename *Aphrodite* was authorized for the remotely controlled missiles on June 23, and the first test flights of the "Mother" control ship and "Baby" robots were conducted the next day. The Baby robot aircraft were initially piloted by a crew of two, and once cruising altitude was reached, remote control was established by the Mother control ship and the robot crew parachuted back to earth over England.

The tests concluded that the concept was practical and *Aphrodite* was put under the control of the 3rd Bombardment Division of the Eighth Air Force. Besides various test aircraft, ten war-weary B-17F and B-17G bombers were earmarked for conversion at the Burtonwood depot. Nine of these were loaded with ten tons of explosives and the tenth with napalm jellied gasoline. The task of conducting the *Aphrodite* missions was handed over to Col. William David's 388th Bomb Group, based at Fersfield. *Aphrodite* missions were scheduled for late July and early August but the need for clear weather led to a string of cancelations. The first mission was launched on August 4, 1944 using two task forces, each with four Mother control ships and two Baby robots. Each robot had two associated Mother control ships with the second having a redundant set of controls in case the first one suffered technical problems. The task forces were supported by USAAF Mosquito reconnaissance aircraft to conduct weather missions in front of the attack group as well as post-strike photography. In addition, close fighter escort was provided by P-38 fighters. The *Aphrodite* mission was preceded by a diversionary bombing mission near the French coast.

A contemporary view of the Schotterwerk Nordwest bunker near Wizernes showing the large concrete dome over the missile assembly chamber as well as the small concrete structure to the left that protected the main venting system. Near misses by Tallboy bombs completely undermined the dome structure, preventing the completion of the facility. It is now a museum called "La Coupole."

The crew of a USAAF Mosquito PR XVI NS559 of the 8th Light Weather Reconnaissance Squadron flown by Lt. Bob Tunnell and photographer Lt. David McCarthy on the August 4, 1944 *Aphrodite* mission when the port engine was damaged by flak, as seen here after returning to base. On August 12, the same crew flew Mosquito NS569 on the ill-fated Anvil PB4Y-1 mission against Mimoyecques where McCarthy was injured when Lt. Joseph P. Kennedy Jr.'s aircraft suddenly exploded nearby.

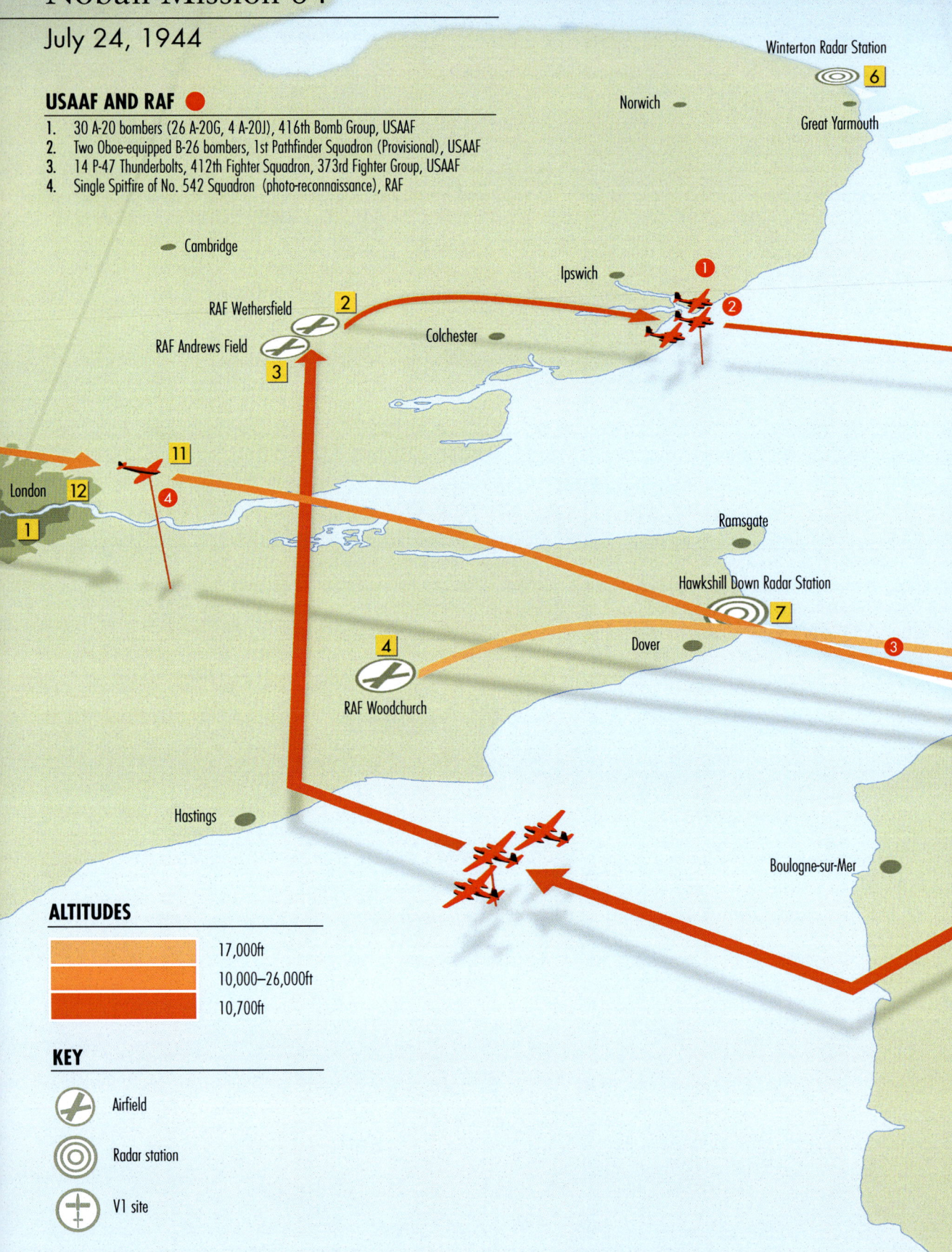

EVENTS

1. The RAF Air Ministry on June 21 determines that foundations for Buildings Q and P at Modified Site Middle-Straete are complete. Site attacked on June 22 by 416th Bomb Group, but results uncertain due to cloud cover. Another mission assigned for July 24.
2. The 416th Bomb Group dispatches 30 A-20 bombers (26 A-20G, 4 A-20J) from RAF Wethersfield (near Braintree, Essex), departing 1000hrs.
3. 1st Pathfinder Squadron (Provisional) dispatches two Oboe-equipped B-26 bombers from RAF Andrews Field (Essex) to lead the two Boxes of 416th Bomb Group to strike Noball Target XI A-149 Middle-Straete.
4. The 412th Fighter Squadron, 373rd Fighter Group dispatches 14 P-47 Thunderbolts from RAF Woodchurch, Kent, to provide air cover for the mission.
5. The bomber mission crosses the coast in the Netherlands south of the Scheldt Estuary. Pathfinders follow "Cat" signal toward target.
6. Winterton Radar Station, serving as the "Cat," tracks the mission over the Channel, following the transponder on the Pathfinder aircraft. The station emits a navigation beam to direct the Pathfinder B-26 to the target.

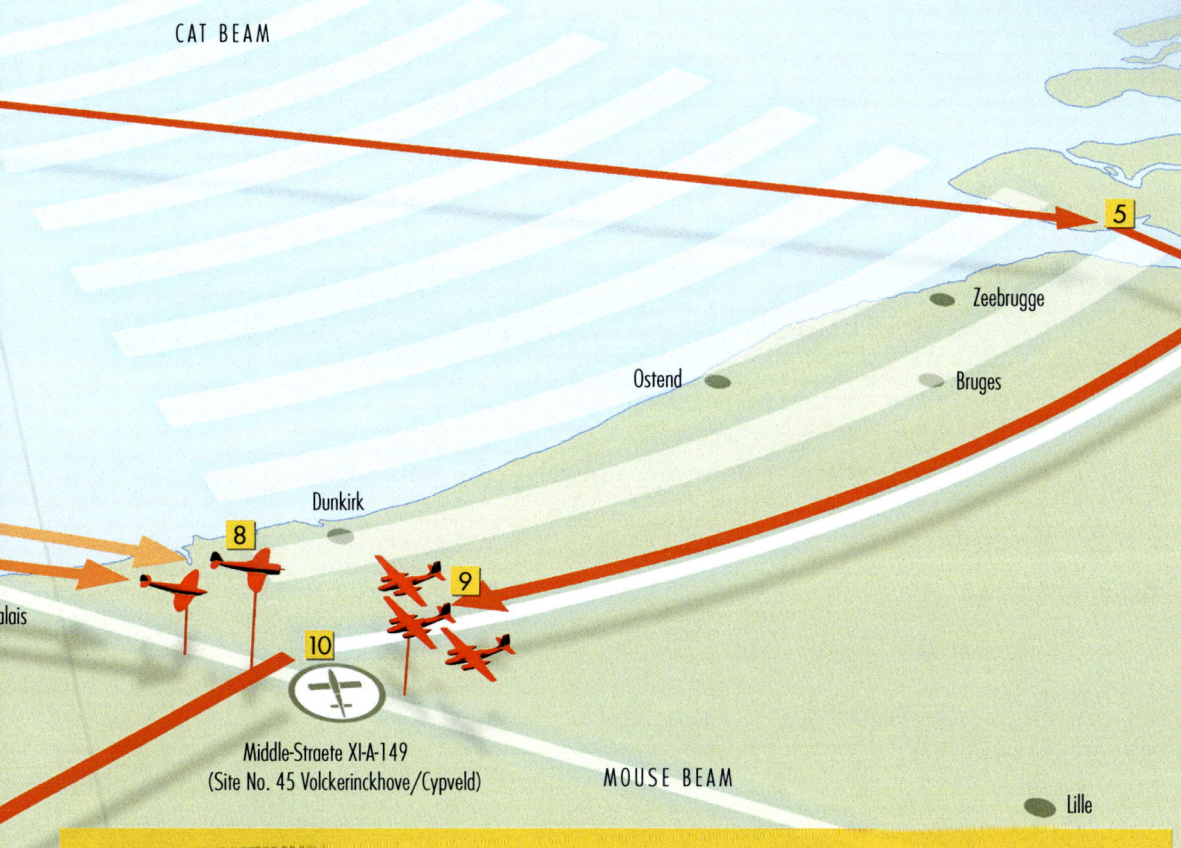

EVENTS CONTINUED

7. Hawkshill Down Radar Station, serving as the "Mouse," emits a beam over the target. The Cat and Mouse beams intersect directly over the target, indicating to the Pathfinder when to begin the bomb drop.
8. At 1045hrs, the fighter escort arrives in the target area at 17,000ft but cannot see the bombers due to cloud cover. The bombers are flying at 10,700ft, and are obscured by the clouds. The Thunderbolts eventually return to base.
9. At 1047hrs, the Pathfinder B-26 leading Box 2 receives the "Mouse" signal from Hawkshill Down, dropping its payload of four bombs. This prompts the Box 2 A-20 bombers to release their bombs as well; one A-20 has bomb release problems.
10. The Pathfinder B-26 leading Box 1 has problems with its Oboe system, but the pilot sees Box 2 ahead dropping its bombs. As a result, he releases his bombs, and Box 1 follows suit. In total, the mission delivers 170 500lb bombs against the target.
11. The RAF sends a Spitfire of No. 542 Squadron based at RAF Benson, Oxfordshire, to photograph the Noball target on the evening of July 24.
12. Photo interpreters at the Air Ministry in London use the Spitfire photos and assess that, "A number of craters are seen within the target area and many in the immediate vicinity. The Launching Point which appears to be incomplete has received four very near misses which have severely disrupted construction. Target is now Noball Damage Category A."

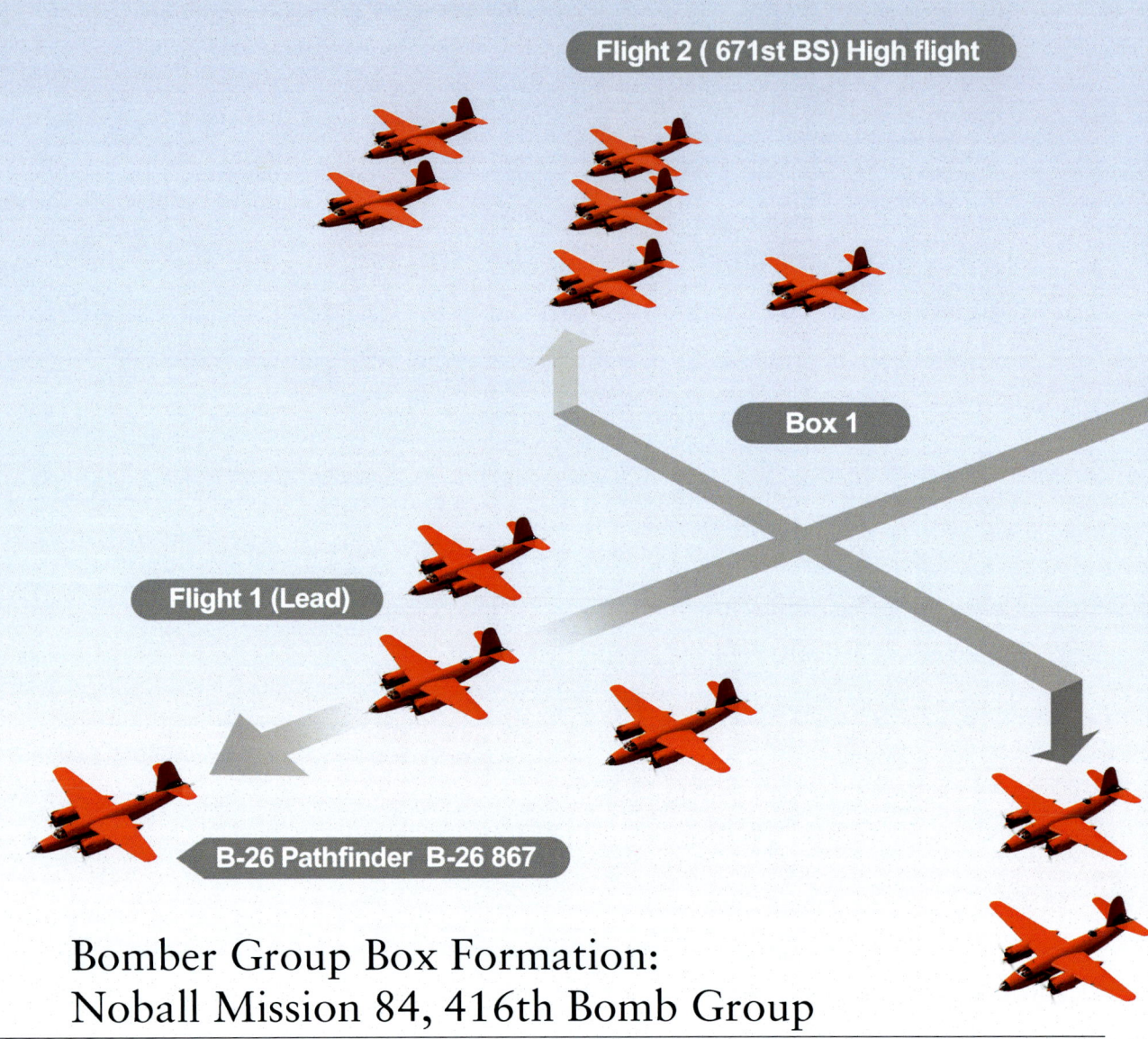

Bomber Group Box Formation:
Noball Mission 84, 416th Bomb Group

July 24, 1944

The medium bombers of the Ninth Air Force generally used a combat box formation during missions over Europe. This was a variation of the system first developed for the heavy bombers of the Eighth Air Force. The box formation was undertaken for several reasons. Since the USAAF conducted daylight missions, the probability of encounters with enemy fighters was higher than for night missions. The box formation was intended to create a compact formation that would maximize the firepower of the squadron, group, or wing against enemy fighters. At the same time, the use of a tight formation increased the likelihood of mid-air collisions due to damaged aircraft, weather conditions, or other contingencies. As a result, the box formation generally employed staggered altitudes both within the squadron as well as within the wing. This illustration shows the typical pattern, with the right squadron serving as high flight, the command element in the lead, and the left squadron as low flight. The introduction of the Oboe navigation aid led to modest changes in the box formation. The Oboe-equipped Pathfinder aircraft from the 1st Pathfinder Squadron (Provisional) would lead a box, with the squadrons following in the usual arrow-shaped box formation. The Pathfinder aircraft would determine the optimum moment to drop bombs based on the intersection of signals from the Cat radar station at Winterton and the Mouse station at Hawkshill, and would provide radio instructions to the squadrons behind. In the event of radio problems, trailing aircraft could see the lead aircraft releasing their bombs, and follow suit. The use of multiple Pathfinders within a group was a common practice due to the technical shortcomings with the Oboe system, as occurred on this mission when one of the two Pathfinders had problems with its Oboe.

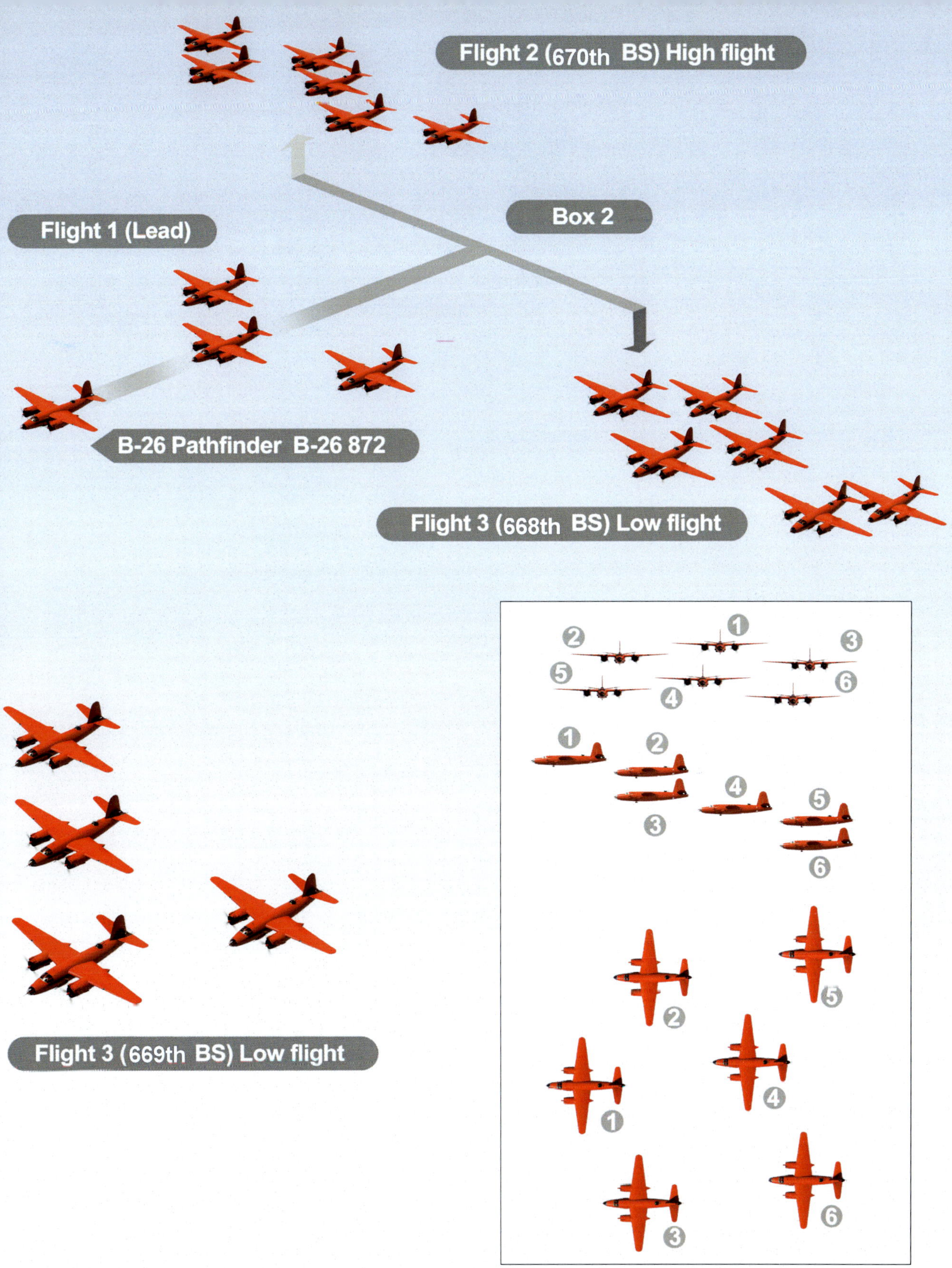

Flight 2 (670th BS) High flight

Flight 1 (Lead)

Box 2

B-26 Pathfinder B-26 872

Flight 3 (668th BS) Low flight

Flight 3 (669th BS) Low flight

SPECIAL ATTACK UNIT 1: TARGET: MIMOYECQUES HEAVY CROSSBOW SITE, AUGUST 12, 1944

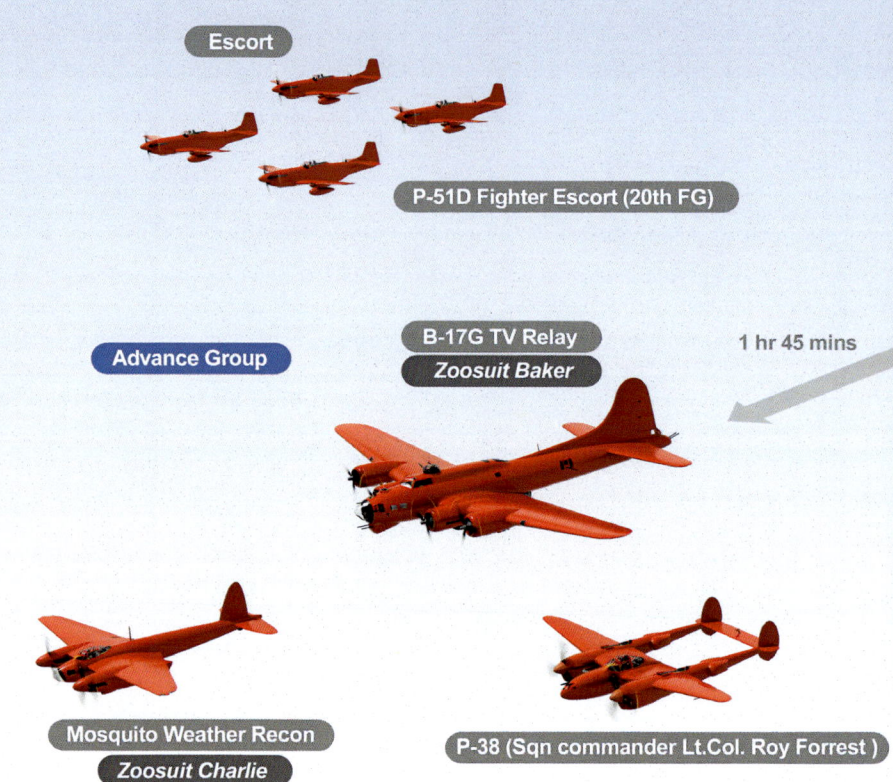

BELOW B-17F "The Careful Virgin" flew with the 323rd Bombardment Squadron, 91st Bombardment Group which began attacking Crossbow targets with the December 24, 1943 mission. This aircraft was retired in May 1944 as a "Weary Willie" and was one of the first ten aircraft converted with Double AZON controls for *Aphrodite*. It was expended as Robot B5 on the first *Aphrodite* mission on August 4, 1944 against the Mimoyecques supergun site, but missed the target.

BELOW RIGHT Gremlin Gus II was one of the first B-17s converted under *Aphrodite* with the Double AZON control system. The associated double set of antennae is clearly evident on the nose. This particular aircraft was later reconstructed with the Castor system and modified to carry a load of special underwater demolition charges for a stillborn attack on the German battleship *Tirpitz*. (Frank A. Law, courtesy of the Burtonwood Association via Aldon P. Ferguson)

Robot B1, intended for Watten, took off as planned and the crew parachuted safely over England. The first attack pass on the Watten bunker was abandoned due to cloud cover and a second pass was made. The B-24 Mother was unable to activate the "Down" control, possibly owing to flak damage inflicted on the aircraft. Robot B1 was flown back out towards the Channel but was hit by flak and exploded before it could be reoriented for another pass.

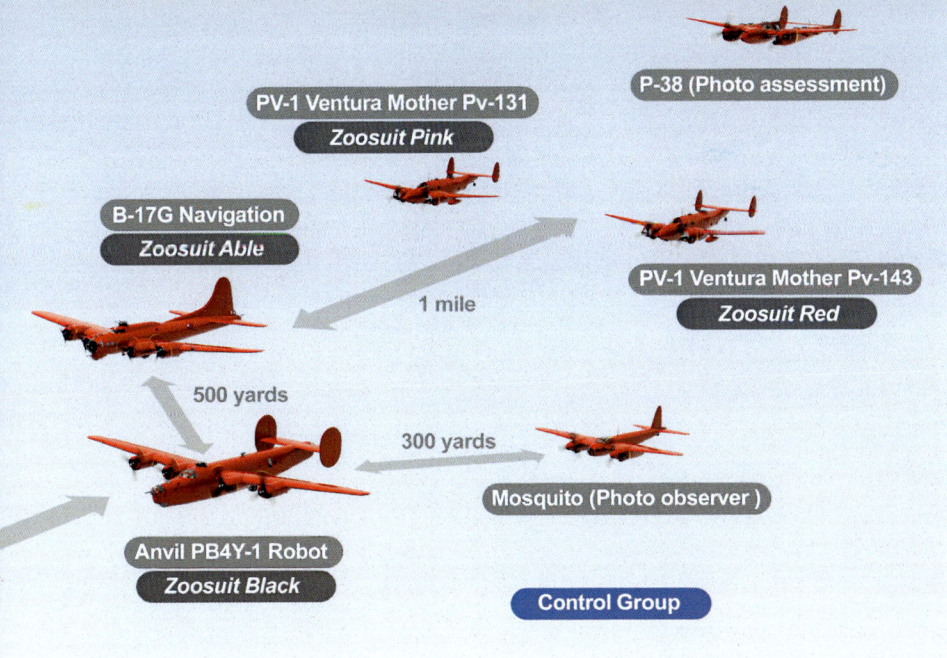

Robot B4 aimed at Wizernes operated satisfactorily and reached the target area. During the final approach, cloud cover momentarily obscured the target and the B-17 impacted about 700 yards beyond the main dome.

Robot B5 was nearly lost when engaged over England by British AA gunners, but the B-17 Mother ship directed it to the target of Mimoyecques. On approach to the target, the Mother crew felt that the robot was flying too high and tried to reduce its altitude to the standard 300 feet. The controls were very crude, and, as a result, the robot impacted about 1,500 feet short of the target.

Robot B8, intended for Siracourt, experienced an altimeter failure over England. One crewman parachuted safely but the aircraft suffered a series on uncontrolled climbs, finally stalling and crashing near Woodbridge.

The failure of the first *Aphrodite* mission led to some changes to procedure. Mission 2 was conducted on August 6 using B-17 Robot No. 1 filled with 10 tons of Torpex explosive and B-17 Robot No. 2 filled with 830 gallons of jellied gasoline and about a dozen 100lb bombs. Both robots became airborne without problem. The Robot No. 1 group encountered a formation of B-24s over the Channel which led to the Mother overshooting the Baby and experiencing control problems. Robot No. 1 went out of control, turned sharply to the left, flipped over on its back, and crashed into the sea. Robot No. 2 seemed to be flying correctly when the crew bailed out, but moments later the Mother noted that the B-17 was drifting to the right. This situation grew progressively worse with the bomber starting to do complete turns. After failed attempts to bring Robot No. 2 under control using the second Mother, the B-17 was deliberately crashed into the ocean rather than risk it inadvertently flying back to England.

The US Navy offered to assist *Aphrodite* using its remote-control technology. The Navy's TDR-1 assault drones had seen their debut near Guadalcanal at the end of July 1944, but these were considered too small for *Aphrodite* since their maximum payload was only one ton. The Navy offered to adapt this remote-control system to the PB4Y-1, the maritime patrol bomber version of the B-24 Liberator bomber. This remote-control system was significantly more sophisticated than the crude Double AZON. The Project Anvil conversions were undertaken at Naval Air Station Philadelphia, and the first Anvil PB4Y-1 and two modified PV-1 Ventura Mother ships departed the United States on July 7, 1944. The Anvil PB4Y-1 was dispatched on its *Aphrodite* mission on August 12, aimed for the Mimoyecques gun site.

The formation became airborne as planned, but before the crew could bail out, the 10.5-ton load of Torpex prematurely detonated, obliterating the Anvil PB4Y-1 south of Halesworth. The massive explosion nearly enveloped a trailing USAAF Mosquito and caused extensive damage on the ground below. The pilot of the aircraft was Lt. Joseph P. Kennedy Jr., son of the former US ambassador to Britain, and elder brother of future US president John F. Kennedy. Further *Aphrodite* missions were halted to determine the cause of the accident. A faulty safe-and-arming system was considered the most likely cause, a conclusion verified by more recent research. The Project Castor systems for the B-17 finally arrived in Britain, but by the time they were ready, Operation *Crossbow* had concluded.

Attacks on the missile industry

Phase II of Operation *Crossbow* placed greater emphasis on attacking the industrial infrastructure of the German missile industry. While this made perfectly good sense, the task was made very difficult by a lack of precise knowledge about the sources for many of the FZG.76 sub-assemblies. By this stage of the war, the Luftwaffe aircraft industry was well aware of the need to disperse the production facilities and the FZG.76 was a good example of this process.

The RAF had knocked out the first FZG.76 assembly plant, the Gerhard Fieseler Werke GmbH in Kassel during a raid on the night of October 22, 1943. This raid was part of the broader battle of the Ruhr, and the RAF was not aware at the time that missile production was under way at that plant. Fieseler eventually transferred some of the production equipment to its plant in Cham, near Regensburg, but this took time due to a shortage of labor. As a result of the Kassel raid, initial FZG.76 production was concentrated at the Volkswagen plant in Fallersleben. This site was identified by the British Air Ministry's Air Intelligence branch in the late spring of 1944, and was placed on the high priority list. It was attacked by the 3rd Bomb Division of the Eighth Air Force on June 20, 1944 with 137 B-17 bombers delivering 305 tons of bombs. The Eighth Air Force eventually raided the plant four times with 581 tons of bombs, with the August 5, 1944 attack being the most destructive. However, the FZG.76 production area took up only a small part of the facility since most of the subcomponents came from elsewhere and the assembly area was located in a well-protected, reinforced-concrete structure. The presses for forming the fuselage were damaged but these components could be supplied from similar presses at the Volkswagen subsidiary plant, codenamed "Elbe" at Schönebeck south of Magdeburg. Final assembly continued at Fallersleben and Schönebeck until February 1945 and the Volkswagenwerke accounted for about two-thirds of the FZG.76 produced. There was some small-scale assembly of the FZG.76 at the Bruns Werke in Köslin near Stettin.

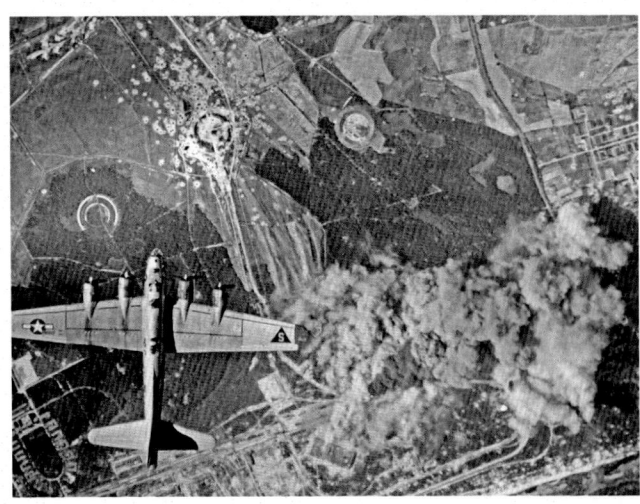

B-17G "Ice Cold Katy" of 612th BS, 401st Bomb Group, piloted by 1Lt. H. Ludeman on Mission 133 on August 25, 1944, Peenemünde. The attacks on Peenemünde in the summer of 1944 were intended to destroy the hydrogen peroxide plant there as well as the Versuchwerke für V-2 workshop as seen here.

The air raids against the assembly plants at Kassel and Fallersleben prompted the Luftwaffe to diversify the assembly effort by starting a major new assembly line in the new underground Mittelwerk II tunnel complex near Nordhausen where assembly began later in October–November 1944. Allied intelligence began to surmise the involvement of the Nordhausen tunnel complex through prisoner-of-war interrogations in the fall of 1944, but the evidence did not become convincing until December 1944. Aerial reconnaissance of the site revealed that the tunnel complex was shielded overhead by 300 feet of gypsum that could not be penetrated by any existing bomb. On December 22, 1944, the British chiefs of staff concluded that a bombing mission against the site was not practical. The status was reconsidered in January 1945 and apparently some consideration was given to attacking the tunnel openings using napalm. Some Bomber Command missions were conducted in the area around the tunnel entrance in April 1945, mainly hitting the labor camps and subsidiary works outside the tunnel. No significant raid was ever conducted on the Mittelwerk tunnel complex itself during the war since it was considered invulnerable to air attack. Total production of the FZG.76 is in dispute but was about 32,780.

Although the bombing raids failed to stop FZG.76 production, they substantially reduced the scale of production. The monthly production objective had been 6,000 missiles per month through September 1944 when Hitler raised the plan to 9,000 units per month. Maximum production was 3,419 in September 1944, after which the total continued to fall to about 2,000 monthly.

FZG.76 SERIES PRODUCTION*												
	Jan	Feb	Mar	Apr	May	Jun	Jul	Aug	Sep	Oct	Nov	Dec	Total
1944	-	76	400	1,700	2,500	2,000	3,000	2,771	3,419	3,387	1,895	2,600	23,748
1945	2,000	2,482	2,027	-	-	-	-	-	-	-	-	-	6,509
*All but 100 of the 2,000 missiles produced in 1943 were scrapped before final assembly due to technical flaws.												

At first, it was presumed that the FZG.76 was powered by a liquid-fuel rocket motor since this was the propulsion system known to be used in the earlier Henschel Hs.293 antiship missile. Signals intelligence from Peenemünde associated FR.155W with the same propellants, T-Stoff (hydrogen peroxide) and Z-Stoff (sodium permanganate). What was not appreciated at the time was that T-Stoff and Z-Stoff were being used by FR.155W for the gas generator used to power the FZG.76 launch catapult. As a result of this misunderstanding, chemical production plants at Peenemünde, Hollriegelskreuth, and Oberraderach were attacked as part of *Crossbow* Phase II. Although thought to produce T-Stoff, the Oberraderach plant in fact produced about 900 tons of liquid oxygen (A-Stoff) per month, associated with the A-4 ballistic missile. During Operation *Eisbär*, a few FZG.76 s crash-landed in Britain without exploding, which allowed Allied intelligence to clarify some of its features such as the use of a pulse-jet engine rather than a liquid-fuel rocket, as used on the earlier Hs.293 antiship missile. As a result, the chemical plants were downgraded in priority.

The Allies refrained from bombing the Mittelwerk missile assembly plant near Nordhausen, partly owing to difficulties in attacking a tunnel complex under a mountain, and partly due to the large slave labor camp near the entrances. This is the entrance to Tunnel A on the south side of the Kohnstein hill. A pile of compressed-air bottles for the V-1 fuel system can be seen near the entrance.

It was presumed that the FZG.76 was guided by use of an inertial platform using gyroscopes. As a result, the Askania plant in Berlin was bombed, along with small facilities thought to be involved in gyro manufacture. A number of other plants were mistakenly associated with FZG.76 production, such as the Opel automobile plant in Rüsselsheim-am-Main and so were on the high-priority list for attack in the summer of 1944.

Under a rain of bombs

Wachtel's FR.155W had 64 launchers available on June 12 at the start of the *Eisbär* offensive, though in practice there were never more than 55 operational on any one day. It was expected that the regiment could launch 3,000 missiles per month. A battery could fire a missile every minute to minute-and-a-half under ideal circumstances. Wachtel later remarked that technical problems at the launcher accounted for about 20 percent of the delays while supply problems associated with the transport system accounted for 80 percent of the problems. The chart here shows the damage inflicted on FR.155W by the *Crossbow* bombing campaign and the number of Allied sorties based on the regimental war diary.

FR.155W OPERATIONAL DATA	Jun 12–30, 1944	Jul 1–15, 1944	Jul 16–31, 1944	Aug 1–15, 1944	Aug 16–30, 1944
Missiles launched	2,450	1,790	1,745	1,381	1,073
Missile crashes	366	201	183	132	133
Daily avg. no. of launchers	40	34	30	33	24
Sites destroyed	2	2	5	0	n/a
Sites heavy damage	22	16	5	11	n/a
Sites medium damage	8	7	6	10	n/a
Sites light damage	10	14	8	8	n/a
Killed	20	15	3	18	n/a
Wounded	71	43	14	53	n/a
Enemy sorties	4,500	3,300	1,350	1,500	n/a
Bombs dropped	18,000	11,500	5,700	6,000	n/a

The first battalion of a second regiment, I./FR.255W had been created at Zempin on June 16, but in practice, this had no effect on the conduct of the summer missile campaign due to the slow pace of its formation and training. As early as May 1944, FR.155W had surveyed launch sites further northeast in Belgium, and the widespread destruction in the Pas-de-Calais led to a gradual activation of these sites to replace damaged sites in France. The first large transfers of batteries began in mid-July due to the amount of damage suffered by the *Crossbow* attacks. By the end of the first week of August, the regiment had suffered so many casualties, and the missile depots had been so badly disrupted that Heinemann's 65.AK headquarters ordered that only three battalions should conduct missile launches and that the other two located south of the River Somme be put in reserve for replacement and maintenance support. At this point, it was estimated that the regiment would receive only about 300 missiles daily. As a result, IV./FR.155W was withdrawn from service on August 8 and III./FR.155W the following day. The days of August 11–16 were set aside for transfers of the two battalions to new launch sites in Belgium.

By mid-August, Allied forces were across the River Seine and threatening the launch areas in the Pas-de-Calais. General Heinemann ordered all surplus equipment moved towards

Two American officers inspect the last functioning V-1 assembly line inside the tunnels of the Mittelwerk complex near Nordhausen.

Antwerp and new bases in the Netherlands. The 65.AK headquarters was moved to Waterloo in Belgium on August 18–19. By the end of August, only I./FR.155W continued to launch missiles, firing its last missile from France at 0400 hours on September 1.

During Operation *Eisbär*, a total of 8,617 V-1 missiles were launched by FR.155W of which 1,052 crashed immediately after take-off, and 5,913 reached Britain. Of these, 3,852 were brought down by air defenses of which 1,651 by guns and the rest by fighters and barrage balloons. So only about 2,300 missiles actually landed in England, about a quarter of those launched.

The FZG.76 was not especially accurate and FR.155W had very limited means to adjust their aim. Postwar assessments estimated their CEP (Circular error probability) at 8 miles (13km) radius, meaning half of all missiles would fall within 8 miles of the aim point, the remainder outside this area. German coastal radars were used to track the flight path of a portion of the missiles, but this did not provide precise information on the point of impact. About seven percent of the missiles were fitted with FuG 23 transmitters which were intended to provide a signal that could be used to triangulate the location of the impacts, but it is unclear from surviving records how effective this proved to be in the summer of 1944. The primary source of accuracy problems was the inherent limitations of the inertial flight control system that relied on a magnetic heading with an associated gyro platform. FR.155W did employ an elaborate weather and atmospheric tracking network in the hopes of compensating for cross-winds and other factors, but this was not especially effective given the state of the guidance technology.

Aphrodite attack on Mimoyecques Heavy Crossbow site, August 12, 1944

During the *Aphrodite* mission against the Mimoyecques Heavy Crossbow site on August 12, the Anvil PB4Y-1 "Zootsuit Black" Robot aircraft was accompanied by a Mosquito PR XVI (NS559) of the 8th Light Weather Reconnaissance Squadron which was filming the mission. The two Mother PV-1 control ships were stationed about a mile behind the Robot. The PB4Y-1 (BuNo 32271) had been modified by the Naval Aircraft Factory at Philadelphia by the removal of unnecessary weight including the gun turrets, the openings being faired over, and the incorporation of a remote flight control system. The Mosquito was flying about 300 yards behind the PB4Y-1 at an altitude of 2,000 feet when the Robot prematurely exploded. The pilot, Lt. Joseph P. Kennedy Jr. and co-pilot, Lt. Willford J. Willy, were later awarded the Navy Cross.

Development of the air-launched FZG.76 took longer than anticipated. This is a test of a pre-series FZG.76 number V83 carried on a Heinkel He-111H-16 during trials from Karlshagen airbase on August 17, 1943. The operational version of this combination mounted the missile under the right wing.

The air-launched missile campaign

Although there had been plans to begin launching FZG.76 missiles from the He-111 bombers of III./Kampfgeschwader.3 at the start of Operation *Eisbär* in June, delays in equipping and training the squadron postponed its start. On July 9, the squadron began attacks on London from Dutch airbases. By July 21, a total of 51 FZG.76 missiles had been launched. On the evening of September 2, 23 were launched against Paris with little effect. By September 5, 1944, when the first wave of attacks ended, III/KG.3 had launched 300 missiles against London, 90 against Southampton, and 20 against Gloucester at a cost of two He-111 bombers. The air-launched missiles were particularly inaccurate; none hit Gloucester and British authorities thought the shots against Southampton had been aimed at Portsmouth! About half the air-launched missiles fell within a radius of 25 miles around the target, which was about three times worse than the ground-launched versions. The rapid Allied advance into Belgium and intense Allied air activity over the Netherlands forced the squadron to withdraw into Germany. At first, the British air defenses did not realize that aerial missile launches were being conducted. But radar began tracking the missiles coming in from the North Sea, and, starting on September 16, the AA gun belt was extended towards Great Yarmouth to deal with the threat.

Operation *Crossbow* ends

The Allied liberation of northeastern France and Belgium in August–September 1944 removed the bases necessary to launch the V-1 missile against Britain. Aside from small numbers of air-launched V-1 missiles, the V-1 missile threat against London ended for the time being. Although Operation *Crossbow* never formally ended, the attention of the Allied bomber forces switched back to the Combined Bomber Offensive against Germany. US Air Force histories usually consider August 30, 1944 to be the end of Operation *Crossbow*.

During fall 1944, the V-1 missile units were re-located to the Eifel region in western Germany and were used against Continental targets, mainly to bombard the port of Antwerp. A new extended-range version of the V-1 missile, the Fieseler Fi-103E-1 that could reach London from launch sites in the Netherlands became available in February 1945. Operation *Pappdeckel* (Pasteboard) began on March 3, 1945 and 275 extended-range V-1s were launched against London through to March 29, 1945. Of these, only about 160 flew any significant distance, 92 were downed by British air defenses, and only 13 reached London, the last on March 28, 1945.

On September 3, 1944, the German Army initiated Operation *Pinguin*, launching two V-2 ballistic missiles from The Hague in the Netherlands against London. The attacks continued at a slow rate, limited by the supply of liquid oxygen. Unlike the V-1 threat, the

V-2 launch sites could not be easily attacked since they were entirely mobile. The German Army deliberately launched the missiles from built-up urban areas along the Dutch coast, expecting that this would restrain the RAF response. RAF fighters strafed the initial launch site on September 9, and the area was subjected to a bomber attack on September 17. During this first phase of Operation *Pinguin*, a total of 43 A-4 missiles were launched, 26 against London and 17 against other targets, mainly in France. For a few weeks, London was spared further attacks after the launch batteries withdrew due to the Operation *Market-Garden* fighting in the Netherlands. Once the fighting around Arnhem tapered off, missile batteries moved back to The Hague and resumed launches against London

The British response to the launches from the Netherlands was measured. The Dutch government-in-exile complained to Churchill about the initial RAF attacks against the missile sites in The Hague because of the collateral damage to residential areas and heavy civilian casualties. There was an eventual understanding between the British and Dutch governments to limit bomber strikes to minimize civilian casualties. For example, the RAF was aware from Dutch resistance that liquid oxygen was being supplied to the missile batteries by eight Dutch plants. However, only one was attacked since the other plants were in mostly residential areas.

Instead, the RAF conducted more than 10,000 fighter sorties flown against rail and road networks near The Hague and Hoek van Holland areas to disrupt missile supplies. The fighters were also authorized to attack launch sites if they were spotted, but this was no easy matter. It was very difficult to target the V-2 launchers since they were usually camouflaged in wooded areas, and the launchers quickly moved after each launch. As a result, few V-2 missile crews were injured at the launch sites by fighter strikes. There was one major exception to the policy of restraint. The use of the Duindigt racetrack in The Hague as a launch site finally became so intolerable that it was heavily bombed in early March 1945, finally forcing the German missile batteries to abandon the area.

Of the 1,359 A-4 missiles launched against London, 1,039 were launched from The Hague and its suburbs while the rest mainly were launched from the Hoek van Holland area. There were 169 (12 percent) failures shortly after launch, 136 (10 percent) disintegrated in the terminal phase of the flight, and 1,054 actually reached England; of these, 517 hit London and its suburbs, only 38 percent of the V-2 missiles launched. Civilian casualties in Britain caused by A-4 attacks totaled 2,754 dead and 6,523 wounded. Although London was the best-known target of the V-2 missiles, Antwerp in fact sustained more attacks.

The A-4/V-2 ballistic missile used an entirely mobile launch system which made it far more difficult for the Allied air forces to target compared to the V-1 cruise missile. This is a test launch conducted in Germany after the war by the British Army using German missile troops as part of Operation *Backfire*.

Hellhound over the North Sea, August 1944

The III./Kampfgeschwader 3 used the Heinkel He 111H-22 which had been converted from H-16, H-20, and H-21 aircraft. The service version carried the FZG.76 under the starboard wing. There was an electrical connection between the parent aircraft and the missile which was used to start the navigation system and to ignite the pulse-jet engine. The aircraft were assigned a specific launch position with a specific heading towards London, but the limitations of the existing navigation system inevitably decreased the accuracy of the air-launched missiles compared to their ground-launched counterparts. Owing to the delays in converting the aircraft and training the crews, III./KG.3 did not deploy to its bases in the Netherlands until late in June 1944, even though the air-launched missile campaign was planned to start simultaneously with the ground-launched campaign. The first missions were flown on the night of July 9, 1944 from Venlo and Gilze-Rijen airbases.

ANALYSIS AND CONCLUSION
Assessing *Eisbär*

The Kraftwerk Nordwest bunker near Watten/Éperlecques is currently preserved as an open-air museum. This is the north side of the complex that was demolished by the first Eighth Air Force raid in August 1943.

The effectiveness of Operation *Eisbär* and Operation *Crossbow* has been questioned over the years, both in terms of the resources employed as well as the results. From a strategic perspective, Operation *Eisbär* was a failure. Hitler's hope that the Vengeance weapons could turn the tide of war was completely unrealistic due to the modest scale of the attacks.

PLANS VS. REALITY		
	V-1	V-2
Planned monthly production	6,000–9,000	900–2,000
Actual peak monthly production	3,420	690
Average monthly production (1944)	2,160	360
Intended maximum daily launch rate*	960–1,440	30–100
Actual maximum daily launch rate	330	26
Intended sustained launch rate (week)	3,360	210
Actual max. sustained launch rate (week)	902	139
*Higher figure includes the Heavy Crossbow sites.		

The monthly production objectives in the summer of 1944 were 6,000 FZG.76 cruise missiles and 900 A-4 ballistic missiles. Even if every missile was successfully launched and struck London, this would have provided a daily capability of about 230 tonnes of high explosive on London per day. By way of comparison, the RAF bomber campaign against the Ruhr industrial region from March 1 to July 31, 1943 delivered, on average, about 1,425 tons (1,300 tonnes) of bombs daily, a nearly sixfold difference. In 1944, the Combined Bomber Offensive delivered substantially more bomb tonnage due to the arrival of the Eighth and Fifteenth Air Forces of the USSTAF. Hitler hoped that Operation *Eisbär* would break the morale of the population of London. Yet RAF Bomber Command failed to break German morale under a far heavier rain of bombs, and it was unrealistic to expect that British morale would collapse under a far weaker blow. Civilian casualties in Britain from Operation *Eisbär* were 5,864 killed and 17,200 seriously injured. About 23,000 homes were destroyed and about a million structures suffered damage.

Allied leaders in December 1943 were very fearful that the German missile attacks would substantially disrupt preparations for Operation *Overlord*. Yet Hitler adamantly refused to allow FR.155W to target the southern ports such as Portsmouth where the invasion fleet was being prepared. If Operation *Eisbär* had started on December 1, 1943 as planned, and if the targeting had been directed against the invasion ports, would this have had a decisive impact on Operation *Overlord*? The answer is probably no. Although it is often forgotten, Antwerp was subjected to German missile attack in the fall and winter of 1944 on a scale very similar to London, since it was the main Allied shipping port for the final advance into Germany. Yet the missile attacks failed to stop maritime traffic in the port both owing to the limited scale of the attacks and also to the inherent inaccuracy of the missiles. The poor accuracy diminished their effects since only a small fraction of the missiles actually struck the port facilities. In the case of *Overlord*, Britain had multiple ports that could have been used to prepare for the invasion, even if ports farther away from France would have been less convenient than Portsmouth and the other Channel ports.

Both the FZG.76 cruise missile and the A-4 ballistic missile were at the bleeding edge of technology in 1944, and their numerous technological flaws substantially undermined the effectiveness of Operation *Eisbär*. The A-4/V-2 missile is ignored in this discussion since the long delays in its development meant that it was not ready in time for Operation *Eisbär*. The FZG.76 suffered from poor reliability due to inherent design flaws and a risky launch system. Of the 8,617 FZG.76 s launched during Operation *Eisbär*, 1,052 crashed shortly after launch, and 1,652 crashed during the course of the flight to England. As a result, more than 30 percent of the FZG.76 missiles crashed before encountering Allied defenses.

The FZG.76 launch system had inherent shortcomings, exacerbated by poor basing decisions in the original "ski site" design. The pulse-jet propulsion system was cheap and efficient but it required some form of launcher system to get the missile up to speed before the pulse-jet could operate effectively. The Luftwaffe selected a steam-powered catapult using a T-Stoff/Z-Stoff gas generator to power the piston. This had two significant technical problems. The use of the volatile mixture of hydrogen peroxide and sodium permanganate was very dangerous to employ in field conditions. There were probably more German missile crew killed and wounded by launcher mishaps than by Allied bombs. The launcher was also at the heart of many of the premature crashes when the gas generator failed to provide enough power to the piston.

Aside from outright technical failures and explosions, the catapult system required an exceptionally long and heavy launch ramp. The Walter Rohrschleuder 2.3 catapult ramp weighed 42 tonnes when fully assembled and was 160 feet (49m) long. It was made up of modular sections, each of which required a truck for transport to and from the depots. Assuming that the launch site had already been prepared with proper concrete foundations, and that sufficient trucks and support equipment were available, the launcher could be assembled or moved in about 18 hours by a well-trained crew, or three to four days for a less-experienced crew. Ideally, FR.155W wanted a fully mobile launch system that could be moved rapidly to avoid Allied air attack and that could be hidden until needed. This proved to be impractical due to the size and weight of the catapult ramp.

The US Army Air Force began manufacturing a copy of the FZG.76 in 1944 as the JB-2 Loon. One of the first changes that was made involved a reconsideration of the launch system. Eventually, a zero-launch system was developed using JATO (jet-assisted take-off) based on several solid fuel rockets, which enabled the launch of the missile from a much smaller ramp. Although Germany had JATO systems in 1943–44, they were mostly based on liquid rocket engines that were not particularly practical for the FZG.76 from both a technical and economic standpoint. Germany lacked the capacity to use solid rocket JATOs like those employed with the JB-2 Loon, since the munitions industry was not capable of mass-producing cast, double-base solid rocket motors. Had this approach been developed, the FZG.76 could have used a mobile basing system that would have been nearly invulnerable to Allied bombing.

Aside from the technical problems with the FZG.76 launcher, the original Stellung-System.1 basing plan was remarkably shortsighted. The Heavy Crossbow sites were an invitation to Allied bombing attack. They were so large and conspicuous that they were attacked long before their completion. Hitler was quite right that the heavy roof construction, as on the U-boat bunkers, was virtually invulnerable to penetration. Even after the Tallboy was introduced in June 1944, there were very few direct hits on the Heavy Crossbow sites that caused fatal damage. However, this ignored the fact that the bunkers could not operate as missile bases since the bombing of roads and rail lines nearby made supply of the bases completely impossible.

The ski sites were constructed in typical military fashion, using a stereotyped pattern with standardized building designs. This was done to make the launch sites more efficient to operate using conscript troops with very limited training. The standardized configuration made the sites particularly easy to spot during construction using aerial reconnaissance, even if many of the buildings were later disguised with camouflage netting. To make matters worse, the sites were constructed by local French construction firms under the direction of Organization Todt, which leaked information of their construction to Allied intelligence. Luftwaffe commanders apparently believed that the sites were so small that they would be ignored by the Allies, especially compared to the massive Atlantic Wall structures being constructed nearby along the coast. When Gen. Heinemann made his first tour of the launch sites, he was flabbergasted at the security risk posed by the French workforce and the obvious vulnerability of the site configuration. If the Luftwaffe had chosen to deploy the FZG.76 in the eventual "modified site" (Einsatz Stellung) configuration, Operation *Crossbow* might not have started until after the initiation of Operation *Eisbär* since the small launch sites would have been invisible until the start of Operation *Eisbär*. The US Strategic Bombing Survey offered an astute assessment of the German missile program:

> In contrast to the Allied "Crossbow" effort, which had an insignificant effect on the prosecution of the war as a whole, the German preoccupation with the development and use of long-range weapons absorbed important quantities of technical ability, labor, materials, industrial capacity and armaments, nearly all of which could have been used to strengthen the flagging defenses of the Reich. This valuable part of Germany's war potential was staked on a race against time and Allied countermeasures. The race was lost and the V-weapon campaign failed – failed to prevent or delay the invasion, failed to shatter Allied morale and failed to change the course of the war.

Assessing *Crossbow*

How effective was Operation *Crossbow* in countering the German missile threat? To begin with, it should be noted that British intelligence organizations, both the photographic reconnaissance efforts and the rest of the intelligence establishment, deserve special recognition for their vital role in discovering the missile threat in the summer of 1943. This provided time for Operation *Crossbow* Phase I to begin well before the start of Operation *Eisbär* and forced the Luftwaffe into modified basing modes that reduced their operational efficiency.

CROSSBOW CAMPAIGN AUGUST 1943–MARCH 1945		
Unit	Sorties	Tons of bombs
US Eighth AF	17,211	30,350
RAF Bomber Command	19,584	72,141
US Tactical Air Forces	27,491	18,654
RAF Fighter Command	4,627	988
Total	68,913	122,133

The *Crossbow* campaign absorbed about 14 percent of all Allied heavy bomber missions from August 1943 to August 1944, and about 15 percent of the medium bomber missions. The diversion of reconnaissance aircraft was greater, absorbing about 40 percent of the missions from May 1943 to May 1944. There has been considerable controversy over the years as to whether the campaign was worth such a large diversion of aircraft that could have been more suitably employed attacking other targets.

To assess this properly, it is necessary to break down Operation *Crossbow* into its two main phases, since the campaign used different forces and different methods during the two periods. Phase I from August 1943 to June 12, 1944 was directed against the Heavy Crossbow sites and ski sites, and was conducted primarily by the heavy bombers of the Eighth Air Force and the two tactical air forces. Phase II started in response to the initiation of Operation *Eisbär* with attacks against the modified sites and eventually shifted the target set to focus on the supply network. Phase II also used a different mix of forces, with substantial participation by RAF Bomber Command, continued missions by the Eighth Air Force, but a diminished role for the two tactical air forces.

Phase I had several significant achievements that diminished the effectiveness of Operation *Eisbär*. To begin with, Phase I effectively destroyed the Heavy Crossbow sites. Had these been constructed as planned, they might have been the single most efficient source of massed missile attacks on Britain. Phase I also destroyed Stellung-System.I, the network of ski sites. In early December 1943 before the attacks, Wachtel reported that he expected to be ready to start the campaign later in the month, and even the more skeptical Gen. Heinemann thought Operation *Eisbär* might be possible in January 1944. By February 1944, the sites had been so badly damaged that the Luftwaffe was forced to modify the launch configuration and create the new Stellung-System.II that was less visible and less vulnerable to Allied bombing attack. There have been criticisms of the continued attacks on the sites in the early spring of 1944, long after Stellung-System.I had been rendered ineffective. Yet it was impossible for Allied planners to anticipate whether the sites could be rejuvenated if the bombing effort had been relaxed.

The main American complaint about *Crossbow* Phase I was the stubborn refusal by the British Air Ministry to try the Eglin attack methods and to continue to rely on missions by the heavy bombers of the Eighth Air Force. This was based on two main premises: that early attacks by medium bombers in December 1943 had been ineffective, and that the low-altitude Eglin-style attacks would have been vulnerable to flak. The ineffectiveness of the early medium bomber attacks was due in no small measure to poor winter weather, which made precision attack impossible. Due to concerns over flak, tactical restrictions to the use of medium-altitude bombing from 12,000 feet also reduced accuracy. Flak did become a problem by the spring of 1944 owing to the increasing number of flak guns added to protect the Pas-de-Calais, but the Stellung-System.I would have been vulnerable to low-altitude attack in the initial months of *Crossbow* when flak densities were still relatively low. The high-altitude attacks by heavy bombers were not especially efficient, and the medium bomber attacks were no better. The only aircraft which demonstrated a high efficiency against the ski sites was the Mosquito, which generally attacked from low altitude as recommended by the Eglin trials.

AIRCRAFT EFFECTIVENESS AGAINST SKI SITES*				
Command	Type	Sorties	Bomb tonnage	aircraft lost
Eighth AF	B-17	116	165.4	1.6
Eighth AF	B-24	217	401.2	2.8
Ninth AF	B-26	218	182.6	0.69
Ninth AF	A-20	331	243.5	1.5
2 TAF	Mitchell	180	219.0	0.87
2 TAF	Boston	535	310.0	5.0
2 TAF	Mosquito	62	39.8	0.87
*Sorties/tons of bombs to inflict Category A Damage.				

Did Phase I delay the start of Operation *Eisbär*? Probably not to a significant extent, perhaps by a month. Although the Phase I attacks certainly did disrupt the creation of the launch sites, serial production of the FZG.76 started so late that it would have been impossible for Operation *Eisbär* to start earlier than the late spring of 1944. From this perspective, the single most consequential bombing attack was the RAF raid on the Fieseler plant near Kassel on October 22, 1943 that shut down the first assembly line. It is not clear that this was decisive in any way, as the serial production version of the FZG.76 was not ready until February 1944 and it is by no means clear that the Fieseler attack contributed to this delay. Other attacks such as the August 1943 attack on Peenemünde do not appear to have had any effect on the FZG.76 program since it was conducted away from the main facilities struck during this mission.

Phase II of the *Crossbow* campaign from June 12 to September 1, 1944 was the most controversial portion of the campaign. The postwar US Army Air Force official history remarked that "The Crossbow campaign of the summer of 1944 must be regarded generally as having failed to achieve its objectives. Indeed, it seems to have been the least successful part of the over-all effort" (Craven & Cate: 1951).

There were several problems at the heart of the Phase II controversy. There was no unified command of the effort due to bitter controversies about control of the strategic bomber force. Although RAF Bomber Command and the Eighth Air Force were supposed to be under the leadership of Leigh-Mallory's AEAF command, personal disputes between Spaatz and Leigh-Mallory led to awkward compromises and frequent disputes that had to be settled by the SHAEF deputy commander, Air Chief Marshal Tedder. As a result, AEAF played little role in directing the *Crossbow* campaign.

Harris was pressured by Churchill into a greater commitment of Bomber Command in Phase II than in Phase I, and indeed Bomber Command carried the main burden in terms of sorties and tonnage. However, Harris remained convinced that the Air Ministry had a poor understanding of targeting, a viewpoint shared by Spaatz and Doolittle. Attempts to create a joint targeting committee under the "bomber barons" made some helpful changes in the focus of Phase II targeting, but arrived at the very end of the campaign and ran up against political interference from Churchill, passed through SHAEF headquarters by Tedder.

Phase II was also hampered by poor intelligence regarding the modified sites and the location of the missile industry. Allied intelligence did learn about the shift to the modified sites as early as February 1944 due to signals intercepts. However, there was no real understanding about the actual configuration of the modified sites. Allied reports about bombing the modified sites in February–May 1944 were in error as the FR.155W regimental war diary makes it clear that none of the new sites was attacked through late May 1944. The modified sites were very difficult to identify properly, due to their minimal structure beyond the launch ramp itself, and the launch ramps were not deployed in any significant number until a week before the start of Operation *Eisbär*. The Allies, especially Bomber Command, staged numerous raids against the modified sites in June–August 1944, but with very modest results. The number of operational launch ramps declined from about 40 in late June to about 33 in early August. There was a significant supply of spare launch rails with about 600 sets having been manufactured during the course of the program. Damaged ramps could be replaced. The modest decline in operational launch ramps did not have a major impact on the overall launch tempo which fell from an average of 135 missiles per day in June to 115 in July in spite of the heavy bombing attacks.

A more egregious problem was the continued targeting of the Heavy Crossbow sites, even though the level of damage evident in the reconnaissance photos should have suggested the impossibility of the use of the sites for missile launches. Yet numerous bomber missions were devoted to attacks on these sites through July 1944.

A later assessment by the US Strategic Bombing Survey (USSBS) concluded that the heavy bombers had a much lower effectiveness against the modified sites than medium bombers, requiring more sorties and more tonnage to inflict Category A damage on a site, while at the same time taking more losses. The Lancaster suffered an unusually high number of losses as these aircraft conducted a significant fraction of their missions at night. Although the Luftwaffe day fighter threat over France had been largely eliminated by the summer of 1944, there was still a robust German night fighter force active nearby. The reasons for the discrepancy in casualties between the Halifax and Lancaster are not evident.

AIRCRAFT EFFECTIVENESS AGAINST MODIFIED SITES (CATEGORY A DAMAGE)			
Type	Number of sorties	Avg. Tonnage	Aircraft lost
B-17	116	191	1.4
B-24	255	415	1.0
B-26	173	188	0
A-20	152	176	0
Halifax	296	997	1.0
Lancaster	220	884	3.0

The Phase II attacks seem to have had the greatest impact when the air commanders in the field forced the Air Ministry to shift the focus of the bombing from the modified sites to the storage sites. The FR.155W war diary attributes 80 percent of the launch problems to missile supply. This included both the Crossbow storage site attacks as well as the general air interdiction/anti-transport campaign being conducted by the Allied air forces in France. The war diary constantly mentions the problem of moving missiles and fuel to the launch sites due to the Allied attacks on roads, bridges, and the railway network.

The extent of damage inflicted on the storage and delivery sites is difficult to determine because of a shortage of records. There were about 11,000 missiles in the pipeline in the summer of 1944, assuming that all production from February 1944 to mid-August 1944 made it forward to the Luftwaffe depots in France; the number may in fact have been smaller. FR.155W managed to launch 8,617 FZG.76 s during Operation *Eisbär*, so the *Crossbow* campaign may have destroyed or stopped the delivery of about 2,400 missiles.

The attacks on the German aircraft industry did not eliminate FZG.76 production though it did reduce it significantly. By 1944, the German aircraft industry had diversified sub-component production sufficiently to make the network resilient to attacks on single plants. Allied intelligence did not have accurate data on the numerous plants involved, and so was able to target only a handful of the main sub-contractors. Although the dispersion prevented a total cessation of production, it was less efficient. The Luftwaffe had planned to reach a monthly production rate of 6,000 missiles monthly in the summer of 1944 when in fact it peaked in the summer at 1,800 due to shortages of material, labor, machine tools, transportation delays, and other problems caused by the Combined Bomber Offensive.

Although Spaatz and Doolittle complained about the diversion of US heavy bombers from the Combined Bomber Offensive to Operation *Crossbow*, in the event, the diversion was not substantial. A compromise was reached early in the campaign to refrain from *Crossbow* missions when weather over Germany permitted visual bombing raids. During the period from December 24, 1943 to August 30, 1944, there were only seven days when the weather in Germany was clear enough for visual bombing but that the Eighth Air Force was diverted to attack Crossbow targets. All of these days were during the summer 1944 Phase II period, and they amounted to 1,869 sorties that might otherwise have been directed against Germany.

In November 1944, the British Air Ministry attempted to calculate the comparative costs of Operation *Crossbow* versus Operation *Eisbär* and concluded that the Allied costs, including damage to London and Allied military expenditures, were about 3.8 times greater than the German costs. As noted earlier, Britain and the United States were far more able to absorb such costs than Germany at this point in the war, and *Crossbow* did not have any significant impact on the Allied conduct of the war. The Allied air forces lost 154 aircraft during Operation *Crossbow* Phase I and 197 during Phase II. Aircrew casualties were 771 in Phase I and 1,462 in Phase II.

One factor that has usually been ignored in accounts of Operation *Crossbow* was the effect on the French civilian population. The Pas-de-Calais region endured about 160 days of Allied bombing raids totaling nearly a quarter-million bombs. About 70 percent of the towns and villages in the region suffered bomb damage to a greater or lesser extent. The damage was somewhat mitigated by the fact that most of the V-1 launch sites were located in rural areas and, in most cases, the Germans forcibly evacuated farmers from the immediate area of the sites. Most of the civilian deaths occurred in the towns near railroad lines and missile storage sites. In total, about 10,000 French civilians were wounded during the bombing raids and about 3,600 killed.

FURTHER READING

Operation *Crossbow* has received considerable attention as part of the general surveys of the Allied strategic bombing campaigns, but there are few books devoted to the campaign. In contrast, there are a large number of books devoted to RAF Fighter Command's actions over Britain against the V-1. Coverage of RAF Bomber Command and Eighth Air Force participation in Operation *Crossbow* is well documented in published accounts. With the exception of Bowyer's history of 2 Group, coverage of the 2nd Tactical Air Force's role in *Crossbow* is by far the weakest of the major commands and Ninth Air Force is not much better. Operation *Eisbär* is not well covered in either English or German-language publications, though the Air Ministry translation of the Kriegstagebuch of Flak-Regiment.155W, located in the library of the Imperial War Museum, certainly helps fill in many gaps. While tactical accounts of V-1 operations are thin, there are ample published accounts of the technical aspects of the V-1, of which the recent Delefosse book is by far the best.

The author consulted a wide range of archival documents in the preparation of this book. The Spaatz papers at the Library of Congress in Washington, DC have extensive documentation on *Crossbow* and Operation *Aphrodite*. Library of Congress also has some intriguing documents dealing with the controversial Eglin Field trials. A variety of record groups were consulted at the National Archives and Records Administration (NARA II) in College Park, Maryland concerning Operation *Crossbow*, including the SHAEF records in RG 331, and USAAF development records in RG18. There are also numerous reports by BIOS (British Intelligence Objectives Sub-Committee), CIOS (Combined Intelligence Objectives Sub-Committee), and CSDIC (Combined Services Detailed Interrogation Centre) which include interrogation of German officials and prisoners of war that help detail the German missile program. The library at the National Air and Space Museum in Washington, DC has a very extensive collection of documents dealing with the V-1, primarily from the technical standpoint.

Government Reports

Helfers, Lt. Col. M., *The Employment of V-Weapons by the Germans During World War II*, US Department of the Army: n.d.

Walter, Gen. Eugen, *V-Weapon Tactics (LXV Corps)*, US Army Foreign Military Studies B-689: 1947

Welborn, Catherine, *V-1 and V-2 Attacks against the United Kingdom during World War II, ORO-T-45*, Operations Research Office, Johns Hopkins University: 1952

n.a., *Aircraft Division Industry Report*, US Strategic Bombing Survey: 1947

n.a., *Gerhard Fieseler Werke Kassel*, Germany, US Strategic Bombing Survey: 1947

n.a., *Handbook on Guided Missiles: Germany and Japan*, US War Department: 1946

n.a., *History of the LXV AK and the V Weapon Campaign*, CSDIC SIR 1641: 1945

n.a., *Investigation of the Heavy Crossbow Installations in Northern France*. 3 volumes, Sanders Mission, *Crossbow* Committee: 1945

n.a., *Kriegstagebuch (War Diary) Flak Regiment 155 (W)*; English Translation by Air Ministry, London

n.a., *Tactical Operations of the Eighth Air Force: 6 June 1944–8 May 1945*, USAF Historical Division: 1952

n.a., *V-Weapons (Crossbow) Campaign*, US Strategic Bombing Survey: 1945

n.a., *Volkswaggonwerke: Fallersleben, Germany*, US Strategic Bombing Survey: 1947

FURTHER READING

Books

Bates, H.E., *Flying Bombs over England*, Froglets: 1994

Bowyer, Michael, *2 Group RAF: A Complete History 1936–1945*, Faber and Faber: 1974

Chevalier, Hugh, *Bombes et V1 sur le Pas-de-Calais*. Les Échos du Pas-de-Calais: 2009

Craven, W.F., and Cate, J.L., *The Army Air Forces in World War II, Vol. III: Argument to VE Day January 1944–May 1945*, University of Chicago Press: 1951

Darlow, Steve, *Sledgehammers for Tintacks: Bomber Command Combats the V-1 Menace 1943–44*, Grub Street: 2002

Davis, Richard, *Carl Spaatz and the Air War in Europe*, Center for Air Force History: 1993

Delefosse, Yannick, *V1: Arme de désespoir*, Lela Presse: 2011

Ducellier, Jean-Pierre, *La guerre aérienne dans le nord de la France: 24 juin 1944, V-1 arme de représailles*, Imp. Paillart: 2003

Flower, Stephen, *A Hell of a Bomb: How the Bombs of Barnes Wallis Helped Win the Second World War*, Tempus: 2002

Freeman, Roger, *The Mighty Eighth War Diary*, Jane's: 1981

Gruen, Adam, *Preemptive Defense: Allied Air Power versus Hitler's V-Weapons 1943–45*, Air Force History: 1998

Hamlin, John, *Support and Strike: A Concise History of the US Ninth Air Force in Europe*, GMS Enterprises: 1991

Hellmold, Wilhelm, *Die V1: Eine Dokumentation*, Bechtermüntz Verlag: 1999

Hinsley, F.H., et al., *British Intelligence in the Second World War, Vol.3, Parts 1 and 2*, HMSO: 1988

Holsken, Dieter, *V-Missiles of the Third Reich: The V-1 and V-2*, Monogram Aviation: 1994

Jones, R.V., *Most Secret War: British Secret Intelligence 1939–45*, Hamish Hamilton: 1988

Murray, Iain, *Dambusters: 1943 Onwards*, Haynes Owners Workshop Manual, 2011

Rust, Kenn, *The Ninth Air Force in World War II*, Aero Publishers: 1970

Saunders, Hilary St. George, *Royal Air Force 1939–1945, Vol. III: The Fight is Won*, HMSO: 1954

Shores, Christopher, and Thomas, Chris, *2nd Tactical Air Force, Vol. 1: Spartan to Normandy June 1943–June 1944; Vol. 2: Breakout to Bodenplatte July 1944–January 1945*, Ian Allen: 2005

Simpson, Bill, *Spitfire Dive Bombers Versus the V2: Fighter Command's Battle with Hitler's Mobile Missiles*, Pen & Sword: 2007

Smith, Peter, *Air-Launched Doodlebugs: The Forgotten Campaign*, Pen & Sword: 2006

Stanley, Roy, *V Weapons Hunt: Defeating German Secret Weapons,* Pen & Sword: 2010

Tedder, Arthur, *With Prejudice: The World War II Memoirs of Marshal of the RAF Tedder*, Little, Brown: 1966

Thomas, Graham, *Terror from the Sky: The Battle against the Flying Bombs*, Pen & Sword: 2008

Webster, Charles, and Frankland, Noble, *The Strategic Air Offensive against Germany 1939, Vol. II: Endeavor; Vol III: Victory*, HMSO: 1961

INDEX

References to captions are in **bold** (with captions in brackets)

A-4/V-2 ballistic missile 20, 49
　Allied discovery of ("P30") 6, 7, **8**, 9
　assembly and erection **21**, 22, **25**, 45, 63, **69**
　basing modes 5
　bases *see under* Wasserwerke launch bunkers
　deployment of 8, 21–22
　development and testing 50–51, 83, 87
　fuel/propellant 9, 21, 44, 77
　first launch 6
　launch/flight failures 50–51, 83
　launch pads **22**, 50, **83**
　missile batteries/crews 50–51, 83
　mobile launch system 83, **83**
　objectives of 5, 30
　operational use 4, 5, 6, 21, 35, 50–51, 82–83, 86
　planned use of 4, 86
　storage and supply 22, 47, 61–62
　transportation of 7, **8**
A-4A/C ballistic missiles 50–51
Air Defence Great Britain 55, 61
Air Ministry 30, 31, 34, 54, 58, 59, 71
　targeting assignments (criticism of) 58, 61, 89, 90, 91, 92
Allied Expeditionary Air Force (AEAF) 13, 34, 41, 54, 59, 90
Allied intelligence-gathering 5, 7, **22**, 47, 48, 51, 53, 54, 58, 76–77, 83, 88, 90, 91
　photographic evidence 6, 7, 8–9, **8**, **9**, 11, 21, 25, **26**, 30, **30**, 32, **43**, **47**, **51**, 53, 59, **66–67**, 69, **70–71**, 88, 91
Aphrodite missions 6, 59, 62, 69, 74–76, **74–75**, 78, (79), **80–81**
Arnold, Gen Henry H. "Hap" 32, 33, 34
A-Stoff 77
Avro Lancaster 8, 9, 14, 15, 29, 39
　B Mk. III **60**
　operations 29, 31, 39, 63, (63), **64–65**, 66, **66–67**, 91
AZON guided bomb 33–34, 69

Backfire, Operation **83**
Belgium 13, 28, 79, 82
　V-1 operations from 5, 11, 34, 78–79, 82, 34
　V-2 attacks on 82, 83, 87
Bodyline Committee 7, 8, 30
Boeing B-17 Flying Fortress 15, 16, 17, 34, **46**, **58**
　B-17F **11**, **45**, **46**, 69, 74, **74**
　B-17G 58, **74**, **75**, 76
　operations 9, **11**, 31, 38–39, **39**, 43, **45**, 58, 61, 69, 74, 75, **74–75**, 76, 90, 91
Brereton, Gen. Lewis 9, 13, 34

Cat/Mouse navigation beams **70–71**, 72
Central Interpretation Unit 7, 30, 33, 34
chemical production plants, bombing of 76, 77
Cherwell, Lord (F.A. Lindemann) 7, 53
Churchill, Prime Minister Winston 7, 8, 53, 83
　role of Bomber Command 56, 90
　and Crossbow sites 30, 54, 56, 57
　anxiety over Heavy Crossbow sites 63
　response to first V-1 attacks 54
Combined Bomber Offensive (CBO) 12–13, 29, 82, 86, 91
Coningham, Air Marshal Sir Arthur 13, 59
Consolidated B-24 Liberator 15, 16
　B-24H **48**
　operations 31, 38–39, 43, **48**, **49**, 57, 69, 74, 75, 90, 91

Consolidated PB4Y-1 69, 75, **75**, 76, 78, (79), **80–81**
"Cookie" Blockbuster bomb 41
Crossbow Committee (UK) 26, 32, 54
Crossbow Committee (US) 32
Crossbow, Operation
　aircraft lost 90, 92
　assessment of 42, 43, 61, 88–91
　criticism of/opposition to 5, 29–30, 53, 56, 57, 59, 61, 62, 88–89, 90, 92
　ending of 5, 82
　Heavy Crossbow targets 6, 28, 29–30, 31, 34, 38, 39, **44–48**, 53, 54, 56, 58, 59, 62, 63, **64–65**, **66–67**, 88, 89, 91
　objectives of 5, 30
　Phase I missions 5, 6, **7**, 9, 13, **15**, **19**, 28, 29–30, 31–32, 35, 38–40, **39**, **40**, 41–42, 43, **43**, 44–48, **44**, 62, 63, 74, 76, 88, 89, 90
　Phase II missions 56–59, **59**, **60**, 61–62, **61**, **62**, 63, **64–65**, **66–67**, 68, 76–78, 88, 89, 90–91, 92
　Plan Eye-Que raid 32
　sorties/bomb tonnages 38, 39, 40, 43, 56, 57, 58, 62, 78, 89, 90
　suspension of (Eighth Air Force) 59
　targeting lists/priorities 58, 61, 62, 76, 78, 89, 90, 91

D-Day/Normandy campaign 6, 11, 13, 29, 30, 32, 39, 40, 41, **47**, 51–52, 53, 54, 55, 56, 59, 87
De Havilland Mosquito 17, 18
　B Mk. IV **41**; FB Mk. VI **42**; PR Mk. XVI **69**, (79), **80–81**
　operations (RAF) 7, **8**, 31, 39, 40, **41**, 43, 63, **66–67**, 89, 90
　operations (USAAF) 69, **69**, 74, **75**, 76, 79, **80–81**
Doolittle, Lt. Gen. James "Jimmy" 12, **12**, 30
　and Operation *Crossbow* 30, 54, 57, 59, 62, 90, 92
　and Project Castor 69
Double AZON control system 69, 74, **74**, 75
Douglas A-20 Havoc **15**, 19, 41, 43, 90, 91
　A-20G **44**, **70–71**, **72–73**
　A-20J **70–71**, **72–73**
Douglas Boston 17, 40, **40**, 90

Eaker, Maj. Gen. Ira **12**
Eglin Proving Ground ("ski site" attack methods) 6, 32–34, **33**, 89
Eisenhower, Gen. Dwight D. (SHAEF) 12, 30, 54, 57, 59, 61
Eighth Air Force
　bomb divisions 16–17, 31, 38: 2nd 39, **48**, **49**, 57; 3rd 69, 76
　bomb groups 16–17: 91st **58**, **74**; 93rd 49; 94th **45**; 100th **39**; 303rd **46**; 388th **11**, 69; 389th 49; 392nd **48**, 49; 401st 60, **76**; 447th 61; 452nd **43**; 486th 51; 492nd **48**
　bomb squadrons: 322nd **58**; 323rd **74**; 360th **46**; 410th **45**; 562nd **11**; 579th **48**; 612th **76**
　bomb wings 16, 17: 1st 9, 45; 4th 9, 16, **45**
　bombing missions 4, 6, 9, **11**, 29–30, 31, 38–39, **39**, 40, 41, **43**, 44–45, **45**, 46, 48, **48**, **49**, 51, 54, 57, 58, 59, 61, 62, 63, 69, **70–71**, 74, 75, 76, **76**, 86, 89, 90, 92
　bombing tactics/techniques 29–30, 31, 38–39, 57, 59
　fighter-escort missions 52, 58

Eisbär (Polar Bear), Operation
　assessment of 86–88
　civilian casualties 87
　plans versus reality 86
　start of 4, 5, 6, 21, 26, 28, 34, 38, 48, 51, 52, 89, 90
　V-1 attacks 35, 52–53, **53**, **54**, 55, **55**, 56, **56**, **57**, 78, 91
England, defensive measures 55, 57
　antiaircraft gun belt/guns 5, 29, 33, 42, 53, 54–56, **55**, **56**, **57**, 61, 75, 79, 82
　barrage balloons 55, 56, **56**, 79
　fighters 5, 19, **19**, 57
Fieseler Fi.103 cruise missile 20, **20**, 82
Fieseler FZG.76/V-1 production 48, 49, 76, 90
FuG 23 radio transmitter 50, 79
FZG.76/V-1 cruise missile
　Allied discovery of ("P20") 7, 8, 9, 11
　codenames for 20
　development and testing 6, 20, 21, 49, 56
　extended-range version 82
　guidance system 25, 49, 78, 79
　manufacture/production of 5, 6, 20–21, 48–49, 54, 76, 77, 86, 90, 91
　powerplant 22, 77, (83), 87
　technical problems 49, **50**, 87
　warhead 37
FZG.76/V-1: launching of 6, 20, 22, 25–26
　electrical commands to (means of) **52**
　final assembly (launch site) 36
　fuel/fueling 22, 25, 27, 37, 52, 53, 54, 77, 87
　gas generator 22, **25**, **27**, **52**, 53, 77, 87
　launch procedure 25, 27
　launch rail (steam catapult) 20, 22, 25, **25**, **26**, 27, **27**, 35, 36, 37, **51**, **52**, 54, 77, 87–88, 91
　launch ramp **4**, 22, 25, **27**, 35, **43**, 47, 52, 53, 87, 90, 91
FZG.76/V-1: operational use 5, 6, 19, 21, 25–26, 29, 35, 52–53, **53**, 54–55, **54**, **55**, 56, **56**, 57, **57**, 61, 78, 82
　air-launches 6, 20, 82, **82**, (83), **84–85**
　assembly/preparation points 25, 36, **36**, 37, 47, 52, 61–62, 68, 76–77, 79
　basing modes/options 5, 25, 34–35, 88
　deployment approval 22
　first and last launches 53, 79
　first mass launch 6
　launch rates 25, 78, 86, 91
　missile losses 49, **50**, 52, 53, 55, 56, **56**, 57, 77, 78, 79, 87
　night launches 52–53, 54, **57**
　planned use of 4
　radar tracking of 53, 55, 79
　storage 25, **28**, 36, **43**, 47, 52, 68
　supply **36**, 37, 38, **38**, 54, 61, 78, 91
　target strike accuracy/success 49–50, 79
　total launches 79
　transport and delivery 34, 35, **36**, 37, 52, 58

Gardiner, Brig. Gen. Grandison 32, 33, 34
German Army (Heer) formations
　65, Armee Korps zbV 26, 28, 34, 35, 52, 53, 78, 79
　Artillerie Abteilung 705 22
　Lehr und Versuchsbatterie 444 50
Germany (targets in) 4, 6, 54, 59, 62
　Ruhr industrial region 4, 48, 49, 76, 87
Gloucester, V-1 attacks on 82

INDEX

Handley Page Halifax 8, 9, 14, 15, 29, 91
   Halifax B Mk. III **61**, **62**
Harris, ACM Sir Arthur 12, **12**, 13, 29, 30
   and Combined Bomber Offensive 29
   and Operation *Crossbow* 30, 39, 56, 59, 90
Hawker Tempest 18, 19
Hawker Typhoon 17, 18, **31**
   Typhoon IB **19**
Hawkshill Down Radar Station **70**, 71, 72
Heinemann, Generalleutnant. Erich 28, 34, 52, 53, 78, 88, 89
   assessment of FZG.76 "light" sites 34–35
Heinkel He-111 82
   He-111H-16 **82**, (83)
   He-111H-20/H-21 (83)
   He-111H-22 (83), **84–85**
Henschel HS.293 antiship missile 8, 54, 77
Hitler, Adolf 4, 5, 20, 35, 53
   and HDP supergun battery 22
   and launch/storage sites 21, 25, 63
   and missile production rates 5, 77, 86, 87, 88
Hockdruckpumpe (HDP) multi-barrel gun 4, 20, 22, **24**, 28, 50, 51
Hydra, Operation 6, 7–8, 21

JB-2 Loon 87–88
Joint Crossbow Committee 61, 62
Joint Crossbow Target Priorities Committee 61
Joint Intelligence Committee 8, 32, 54
Jones, R.V. 8

Kennedy, Lt. Joseph P. Jr. 69, 76, (79)

launch sites (FZG.76/V-2) 11, 25, **28**, 37, 52, 53, 78, 82
   bombing of 28, 38–39, 51, 56, 58, 59, 61, 62, 63, 68, **70–71**, **72–73**, 78, 89, 90–91
   construction/features 9, 11, 25, 28, 34–35, 35–36, 52
   damage assessment 78
   flak defenses 28, 51
   intelligence on 11, 35, **51**, 58
   location/numbers of 11, **23**, 25, 92
   old ("light") **23**, 25, 34, 35, 51, 88, 89
   see also "ski sites"
   new ("modified") **23**, 35–36, **35**, **51**, 52, 53, 58, 62, **70–71**, **72–73**, 88, 89, 90–91, 92
Leigh-Mallory, ACM Sir Trafford (AEAF) **13**, 34, 41, 54, 90
Leopold FZG.76/V-1 missile depot 37, 52, 62, 68
liquid oxygen, production/use of 9, 21, 44
Lockheed P-38 Lightning 18, 19, 34, 58, 69, **74**, **75**
Lockheed PV-1 Ventura 75, **75**, 79
London, attacks on 22
   V-1 4, 5, 6, 11, **23**, 25, 28, 29, 49–50, 52–53, **53**, 54–55, **54**, **55**, 56, **56**, 82, (83), **84–85**, 86, 87
   V-2 4, 6, **23**, 25, 28, 82–83
Luftwaffe formations (air) 4, 8, 26, 47, 53, 62, III./KG.3 82, (83), **84–85**
   IX.Fliegerkorps 53
   10.Flieger-Dvn 26
   bombing operations 4–5
   fighter force 9, 13, 20, 29, 42, 45, 49, 54, 88, 89, 91
   Luftflotte 3 4–5
Luftwaffe formations (flak) 25, 26, 28
   FR.155(W) 6, 8, 25–26, 31, 37, 38, 42, 49, 51–52, 53, 55, 57, 61, 62, 77, 78, 79, 87, 90, 91;
   I. Abt. 6, 26, 28, 37, **39**, 79; II. Abt. 28, 31, 37, 42, **51**; III. Abt. 28, 37; IV. Abt. 6, 28, 37, **43**, 53, 78
   FR.255(W) 37: I. Abt. 78
   launch batteries/sections/troops 25, 49, 52, 53

Market-Garden, Operation 83
Martin B-26 Marauder 15, 19, 34
   B-26C **44**

operations 32, 41, 43, **44**, 46, 90, 91
Pathfinder aircraft **70–71**, **72–73**
Mayer, Hans Ferdinand (physicist) 7
McCarthy, Lt. David **69**
MI6 (Scientific Section) 8
Mimoyecques HDP gun site 22, **23**, 45, 46, 51, 63, 68, **74–75**, 75–76
   bombing of 31, 45, 46, 63, 68, 69, 74, 75, **74–75**, 75–76, (79), **80–81**
Mittelwerk assembly plant 76–77, **77**, 79

napalm jellied gasoline 69, 77
Netherlands, V-1/V-2 attacks from 5, 79, 82–83
Ninth Air Force 9, 13, **57**
   aircraft **7**, 13, 15, **15**, 31, 32, 34, 41, 43, **43**, **44**, 58
   bomb groups 19: 322nd **7**; 387th **44**; 416th **15**, **44**, **70–71**, **72–73**
   bomb squadrons 13: 449th **7**; 558th **44**; 668th **72–73**; 669th **44**, **70–71**; 670th **72–73**; 671st **72–73**
   bomb wings 19, 41
   fighter groups 18, 19, 41: 55th 58; 373rd **70–71**
   fighter squadrons: 412th **70–71**
   fighter wings 18, 19
   operations **7**, 13, 15, **15**, 30, 31, 32, 34, 41, 43, **43**, **44**, 46, 54, 56, 58, **70–71**, **72–73**, 89, 90
Noball missions **9**, **10**, 15, **26**, 30, 31, 34, 35, 38–39, **39**, 40, 40, 41–42, 43, **43**, **44**, **51**, 51, 58, 62
   categories of damage (A–D) 32
   Mission No. 84 **70–71**, **72–73**
   Mission No. 164 (Plan Eye-Que) 32
   Mission No. 221 11
   Mission No. 280 **43**
   RAF/USAAF assessment of 32
   sorties/bomb tonnages 40, 41, 42, 62
Nordpol FZG.76/V-1 missile depot 37, 52, 61–62
North American Mitchell 17, 40, 48, **59**, **60**, 90
North American P-51 Mustang 17, 18, 19, 31

Oberkommando der Wehrmacht 26, 28, 34
Oboe navigation aid **70–71**, 72
Organization Todt 21, 25, 35, 45, 46, 88
Overlord, Operation 13, 32, 40, 51–52, 54, 87

Pappdeckel, Operation 82
Paris, V-1 attacks on 82
Pathfinder aircraft 23, **66–67**, **70–71**, **72–73**
Peak, Flt Sgt E.P.H. (Mosquito pilot) 8
Peenemünde development center 11, 21, 25, 77
   Allied intelligence-gathering 6, 7, **8**, 21
   bombing of 6, 7–8, 21, 76, 90
   chemical production 77
   missile development work 6, 7, **8**, 21
   missile test sites 21: P-7 **8**
Pinguin, Operation 82–83
Pointblank, Operation 13, 29, 30, 41, 42, 54
Plymouth, V-1/V-2 threat to **23**
Portsmouth, V-1 threat to 11, **23**, 32, 53, 82, 87
Project Anvil 75, 76, (79), **80–81**
Project Castor 69, 74

RAF 2nd Tactical Air Force
   aircraft 12, **31**, 32, 40, **40**, **42**, 43, 59, **59**, **60**
   Crossbow operations 13, 30, 31, 32, 40, **40**, 41, 59, **59**, **60**, 62, 89, 90
   groups 17–18: 2 13; 83 13; 84 13; 85 **19**
   Normandy campaign 41, 54, 56, 59
   squadrons 13, 17–18, **31**, **42**, **59**, **60**: 56 **19**; 107 **40**; 180 **60**; 193 31; 302 (Polish) **39**; 320 (Dutch) **40**; 487 (RNZAF) **42**
   wings 17–18: 140 **42**
RAF Bomber Command
   aircraft 14–15, 17, 34, 39, **41**
   bombing missions 4, 6, 7–8, 12–13, 21, 22, 29, 31, 39, 48, 49, 59, 60, 61, 62, **62**, 63, (63), **64–65**, **66–67**, 68, 76, 77, 83, 87, 89, 90–91
   groups: 1 14; 2 **41**; 3 14; 4 14; 5 14–15; 6 (RCAF) 15, **61**, **62**

squadrons 14–15, 29: 75 31; 425 (RCAF) **61**, **62**; 487 (RNZAF) **42**; 514 **60**; 617 29, 31, 48, 54, 63, (63), **64–65**, **66–67**, 68
RAF Fighter Command 5, 63, 89
   groups: 11 **66–67**
   squadrons: 80 **66–67**; 229 **66–67**; 274 **66–67**; 302 (Dutch) **39**; 542 **66–67**, **70–71**
rail/road networks, attacks on 38, 41, 52, 54, 58, 62, 83, 88
Republic P-47 Thunderbolt 18, 19, 31, 34, **70–71**
resistance groups/networks 7, 11, 83
Richard FZG.76/V-1 assembly depot 62, 68
Royce, Maj. Gen. Ralph **57**

Sandys, Minister of Supply Duncan 7, 8, 11
SHAEF 54, 57, 61, 90
Short Stirling 17, 29, **29**, 31, 39
"ski sites" 28, 29, **33**, 36, 87, 88, 89
   Allied identification of 9, 11
   bombing of 19, **26**, 30, 31, 32, 33–34, 38–39, **39**, **40**, 41, 42, 43, **43**, **44**, 54, 58, 59, 62, 89
   construction/features of **9**, **10**, 11, **26**, 30, 36, 88
   damage assessment 42, 43
   flak defenses of 19, **49**
   intelligence on **9**, **26**, 30, 33, 53, 88
   locations of **23**, 31, 32, 42
   stereotyping of 9, **10**, 88
slave labor, use of 77
Southampton, attacks on 53, 82
Spaatz, Gen. Carl 12, 13, 30, 34, 54, **57**, 59
   and Operation *Crossbow* 29, 30, 54, 61, 62, 90, 92
   and Operation *Pointblank* 29
Steinbock, Operation ("Baby Blitz") 4–5
Sullivan, 1Lt. Dan **11**
Supermarine Spitfire 17, 18, 43
   fighter-escort sorties 32, **39**
   photo reconnaissance sorties **24**, **70–71**
   Spitfire IX **39**, 63, **66–67**

Tallboy super-heavy bomb 6, 48, 54, 62, 63, (63), **64–65**, **66–67**, 68, **68**, 69, 88
Tedder, ACM (SHAEF) 54, **57**, 59, 61, 62, 90
Torpex high explosive 75, 76
T-Stoff 22, 27, 54, 76, 77, 87
Tunnell, Lt. Bob **69**
Twining, Maj. Gen. Nathan F. 12

US Navy **28**, 75
US Strategic Bombing Survey 88, 91

Vickers Wellington 17
Volkswagen FZG.76/V-1 production 76

Wachtel, Oberst Max (FR.155W) **20**, 25, 28, 51, 52, 78, 89
Wallis, Barnes 48
War Cabinet 53, 54, 55, 61, 63
Wasserwerk launch bunkers 46–47, 82, 83
   Cherbourg B8 (Martinvast) 25, 31, 46
   Desvres (Lottinghen) **23**, 25, 45, 47
   No. 2 (Ölkeller Cherbourg) 47
   Valognes B7 (Tamerville) 25, 46
Watten (KNW) A-4/V-2 launch bunker 9, 21–22, **21**, **23**, 44–45
   bombing of 6, 30, 44–45, **45**, 46, **47**, 48, 63, 68, **68**, 74, 86, **86**
Wizernes (SNW) A-4/V-2 launch bunker 9, 21, 22, **22**, **23**, **25**, 45, 63, 69
   bombing of 63, (63), **64–65**, 66, **66–67**, **69**, 75
Siracourt (Saint Pol) **23**, 25, **30**, 45, 46, 47, **49**, 63, 75
Winterton Radar Station **70**, 71, 72

Zapp, 2Lt. Robert **11**
Zempin training site 6, 8, 11, 25, 49, 78
Z-Stoff 22, 27, 53, 77, 87